THE MACROECONOMY

T

THE NEW ZEALAND
MACROECONOMY

A BRIEFING ON THE REFORMS

THIRD EDITION

PAUL DALZIEL
RALPH LATTIMORE

OXFORD
UNIVERSITY PRESS

OXFORD
UNIVERSITY PRESS

540 Great South Road, Greenlane, New Zealand

Oxford University Press is a department of the University of Oxford.
It furthers the University's objective of excellence in research, scholarship
and education by publishing worldwide in

Oxford   New York
Athens   Auckland   Bangkok   Bogotá
Buenos Aires   Calcutta   Cape Town   Chennai
Dar es Salaam   Delhi   Florence   Hong Kong
Istanbul   Karachi   Kuala Lumpur   Madrid   Melbourne
Mexico City   Mumbai   Nairobi   Paris   Port Moresby
São Paulo   Singapore   Taipei   Tokyo   Toronto   Warsaw
and associated companies in
Berlin   Ibadan

OXFORD is a trade mark of Oxford University Press

ISBN 0 19 558402 3

Edited by Cathryn Game
Cover design by Heather Jones
Typeset by Desktop Concepts P/L, Melbourne
Printed by Kin Keong, Singapore

CONTENTS

TABLES

GRAPHS

PREFACE

In the opening lecture of the first-year macroeconomics class at Lincoln University, our students are told that the first step in macroeconomics is to define and describe the key variables that are the object of our study. Only when we understand what is meant by real per capita gross domestic product (GDP), the terms of trade, unemployment, inflation, the balance of payments, the real exchange rate and so on, and only when we know how they have behaved over time, is it sensible to begin putting together macroeconomic models that seek to explain their behaviour. Then we can use these models to provide policy advice.

Recognition of this principle led us in 1991 to publish *A Briefing on the New Zealand Macroeconomy, 1960–1990*. That small book of twenty graphs and sixty pages was designed to meet the need for a single, comprehensive source of New Zealand macroeconomic data. Its title and format were based on an earlier booklet produced by government economists at the time of the Economic Summit Conference in 1984. The first part of the book presented the time series in graphs, the second part presented a brief commentary on New Zealand's economic experience over the previous thirty years, and the third part presented the data in an appendix table.

Even as that booklet was being published, however, the New Zealand Government was implementing the final stage of a programme of economic reform that had commenced in the second half of 1984. Indeed, in the decade 1984–94, every aspect of New Zealand's economic policy was subject to radical change, from the decision to float the New Zealand dollar in March 1985 to the passing of the Fiscal Responsibility Act in June 1994. Each component of the reform process has had its critics, and indeed the whole programme of reforms has been denounced in some quarters as a foreign ideology imposed by successive governments too isolated from popular opinion under New Zealand's former first-past-the-post electoral system. On the other hand, the reforms have attracted considerable international attention and acclaim, as well as receiving strong support from other domestic interests, for the way in which the orthodox economic model of market-based development has been consistently applied across such a wide range of policy areas.

Reflecting on this debate, it seems to us important that both advocates and critics of the reforms, as well as those responsible for guiding economic management over the next decade and longer, should not lose sight of New Zealand's actual experience as recorded in its macroeconomic data, for a number of reasons.

First, it is only by considering New Zealand's economic performance in the two decades before 1984 that one can appreciate why there was so much pressure for change. The reform process was not initiated from overseas, but grew out of a widespread recognition that New Zealand was suffering from severe imbalances in its fundamental macroeconomic indicators (the fiscal deficit and the balance of payments, in particular), and that this was reflected in slow economic growth rates and rising unemployment.

Second, advocates of the reforms tend to downplay the extent of the sacrifices made during the reform process, some of which still endure. The data reveal that New Zealand suffered a very long recession (about eight years) during the implementation and transition phases of the programme, producing very high unemployment and an increase in visible poverty which still shocks many New Zealanders.

Third, critics of the reforms tend to downplay the successes that emerged around 1993. The data reveal that price stability has been maintained, for example, and that a strong fiscal deficit after years of chronic deficits allowed a double round of tax cuts in 1996 and 1998. Further, these successes took place during a period of sustained growth that would have astounded policymakers in the 1970s and early 1980s, although the Asian currency crisis in 1997/98, combined with extensive domestic droughts, revealed New Zealand's continuing vulnerability to external and internal economic shocks.

Finally, it seems to us equally mistaken to think either that New Zealand can turn back the clock on the reforms or that all economic and social problems have been solved during the reform process. For better or for worse, the infrastructure of the reforms is now firmly cemented into place, so that future economic management in New Zealand must build on their successes without ignoring any of their failures and weaknesses. Again, examination of the actual data provides a guide to policy issues requiring further work.

In 1996, therefore, we updated our earlier book in a new format that integrated the graphs and the economic commentary within chapters based on the major areas of New Zealand's policy reforms. In this new format, preserved in this third edition, the graphs are still accompanied by a brief description and references to data sources for each time series, but they are presented within the context of the role they played in the programme of reforms, and of the economic principles used by policy advisors as they designed each particular reform. The final chapter then reflects on the ongoing issues raised by New Zealand's experience, particularly since the end of the reforms in 1994.

In preparing this third edition, we have updated all of the graphs to 1997/98 (although most of the final year's data must be considered as provisional) and have taken the opportunity to revise some of the graphs in the light of recent developments. Readers will notice, for example, that the graphs of chapter 2 no longer compare New Zealand's key macroeconomic indicators with averages for OECD small countries. This is because OECD now includes Mexico in its small country data set, which has produced a large structural break in that data series. Instead, chapter 2 introduces comparisons with Australia, reflecting what is becoming a common practice on both sides of the Tasman when arguing about the different economic policies of the two countries since 1983/84. Graph 6.2 has also been changed, depicting 'social security' rather than 'social welfare benefits' government spending. The new series emerged as an important statistic in the government's 1998 promotion of its consultation aimed at developing a Code of Social Responsibility, and also facilitates a discussion of trends in New Zealand's welfare state since the 1960s. Finally, readers are advised that there was an unfortunate calculation error in the real exchange rate series (graph 4.1) in the previous edition. That error has been corrected, but this series remains problematic and readers should treat the real exchange rate data as indicative only.

Writing the text has been an interesting experience for us. By reputation, one of us is a strong critic of aspects of the reforms, the other a strong advocate of the programme's basic principles. At the start of this project, we agreed that we would not publish anything we could not both support, and we have been surprised by how easily we were able to resolve the few differences that emerged. This is in large measure due to our approach of allowing the data to speak for themselves, so that readers are left to make their own judgments about the overall success of the reforms, and the value of each component of the programme.

We are pleased to acknowledge again the generous assistance we received in preparing earlier editions of this book, particularly from Geoff Bertram, Simon Bradbury, Alison Carew, Brian Easton, Peter Harris, Andrew Turner, and our colleagues in the Commerce Division at Lincoln University. Our publisher, Linda Cassells, has again been very helpful and encouraging in bringing this book to completion, and we are grateful to our editor, Cathryn Game, for her careful attention to some details we had missed. We apologise for any errors or omissions that may remain in the material that follows, but would welcome any comments readers may care to send us.

Paul Dalziel
Ralph Lattimore
dalzielp@lincoln.ac.nz
lattimor@lincoln.ac.nz
Commerce Division
www.lincoln.ac.nz/comm/
P.O. Box 84
Lincoln University
Canterbury
NEW ZEALAND

A WORD ABOUT GRAPHS

This book contains twenty-eight graphs depicting forty-two different macroeconomic time series data relevant to the New Zealand economy. Before proceeding to present and discuss these data, it may be worthwhile to review briefly some features of different graph types.

THE HORIZONTAL AXIS

The horizontal axis of every graph in the first eight chapters measures the years from 1959/60 to 1997/98. Unless otherwise noted, the data all refer to the 'financial year'; that is, to the twelve months from 1 April in the previous year to 31 March in the current year. On 18 July 1984, for example, the New Zealand dollar was devalued by 20 per cent, and this is recorded in the relevant data series for the year ending March 1985 (written in the text as 1984/85). The major exception to this rule is data relating to the government's 'fiscal year'. Traditionally, the fiscal year also referred to years ending in March, but in 1989 the government moved its fiscal year to end in June. Thus April, May, and June 1989 were treated as a transitional quarter, and the public accounts for 1989/90 were for the year ending 30 June 1990.

When looking at the horizontal axis it is also important to distinguish between the data that record 'flows' and those that record 'stocks'. Flows are economic activities that take place over a period of time; for example, GDP and the fiscal deficit. Stocks are items whose values are determined at some moment in time; for example, the rate of unemployment or the level of public debt. The horizontal axis will state the period of time for flows (for example, a financial or fiscal year), but for stocks it will state either that the graph is showing an average value over a period of time (as in the case of unemployment in graph 2.3) or that it is showing the value at some precise moment in time (normally the end of the financial or fiscal year, as in the case of public debt in graph 6.3).

As well as quantities, some of the graphs depict different price series; for example, the terms of trade and the interest rate. In these cases the label on the horizontal axis states whether the graph is showing average values over the financial year or actual value at a particular time of the year (usually the end of March).

In chapter 9, there are four graphs that use quarterly data (that is, values for three months at a time). In these graphs, the horizontal axis labels the March quarter data with the relevant year.

THE VERTICAL AXIS

The vertical axis explains what type of graph it is. There are three types. The first is for a series showing levels; for example, real per capita GDP in graph 1.1. If this type of graph is sloping upwards at some point, this means that the statistic is growing; if it slopes downwards, the statistic is shrinking. The graphs showing index levels are a special case; for example, the terms of trade index in graph 1.2. In index graphs, the unit of measurement is defined so that the index can be set at 100 in an arbitrarily chosen base year, and the graph shows how the value of the statistic rises and falls over time, compared to its value in that year.

The second type of graph measures the percentage change of a statistic; for example, graph 2.1 depicts the percentage change in real GDP, and graph 2.2 depicts the percentage change in the GDP deflator. If the level of the underlying statistic is growing, the graph will show positive values for the percentage change; if the values are negative, it means the underlying statistic is shrinking.

The third type of graph measures the percentage share of a statistic; for example, graph 2.3 depicts unemployment as a percentage share of the labour force. If such a graph slopes upwards, it means that the share of the statistic is increasing; that is, it is growing faster (or shrinking less slowly) than the other components of the item being partitioned.

CHAPTER ONE

INTRODUCTION TO THE
NEW ZEALAND ECONOMY

New Zealand can be described as a small trading nation whose average income level places it among the richest 20 per cent of countries in the world. Historically, New Zealand's wealth rose out of its special trading partnership with the United Kingdom, which allowed it to export large quantities of agricultural products to that country at favourable prices. The proceeds from those exports were used to purchase the capital equipment and raw materials needed to expand a domestic manufacturing sector protected from international competition by an extensive system of import licensing and high tariffs. As the UK began to move towards greater integration with Europe in the 1960s, this special trading partnership began to weaken until, on 1 January 1973, the UK's entry into the European Economic Community (now the European Union) signalled its end. That same year, the first oil shock tripled the price of one of New Zealand's most significant imported raw materials. These two events substantially changed New Zealand's economic environment, and a large part of this book will be devoted to explaining and evaluating the economic reforms introduced by subsequent governments to cope with these changes.

THE STRUCTURE OF THE NEW ZEALAND ECONOMY

The starting point for any discussion by economists about economic performance is an evaluation of the country's gross domestic product (GDP). Because GDP estimates the value of goods and services produced within a country during a particular time period, inspection of the components of GDP reveals the underlying structure of that economy. Table 1.1 shows New Zealand's GDP for the year ending March 1995.

There are three parts to the determination of GDP, as is shown in table 1.1. The first part estimates total market production in the economy. This is

Table 1.1   Gross domestic product by production group for the year ending
             March 1995

Market production groups	$ million
Agriculture	4,852
Fishing, hunting, forestry, logging, and mining	2,671
Manufacturing	16,029
Electricity, gas, and water	2,327
Construction	3,048
Distribution	13,853
Transport, storage, and communication services	7,111
Finance, insurance, real estate, and business services	12,746
Ownership of owner-occupied dwellings	6,603
Community, social, and personal services	4,034
LESS: Bank services charges not allocated	–3,145
Non-market production groups	
Central and local government services	8,820
Private non-profit and domestic services	1,025
TOTAL PRODUCTION	79,974
PLUS: GST on production	5,710
PLUS: Import duties and other indirect taxes	893
GROSS DOMESTIC PRODUCT	86,577
Divide by New Zealand mean population (millions)	3.541
PER CAPITA GROSS DOMESTIC PRODUCT (DOLLARS)	24,450

Description
Gross domestic product (GDP) estimates the total value of goods and services produced in New Zealand during a given time interval. Note that GDP is not a precise measure of social welfare because it excludes some production that is not sold in markets (for example family care) and some costs of production (for example pollution). The table shows the value of New Zealand's GDP for the year ending March 1995, analysed by type of production. Statistics New Zealand uses twenty-five production groups, but some of the smaller categories have been combined in the table to give ten Market Production Groups and two Non-Market Production Groups. The table also shows three adjustments needed to obtain the total value of production (subtracting bank services charges not allocated to individual production groups, adding the goods and services tax, and adding other indirect taxes such as import duties). Per capita GDP is obtained by dividing GDP by the country's mean population. This can be interpreted as the average income produced in New Zealand during 1994/95.

Sources
Analysis of gross domestic product by production group comes from table 2.1 of *New Zealand System of National Accounts 1997*, published by Statistics New Zealand. The figure for mean population comes from Statistics New Zealand's INFOS series DPEA.SBIC.

the production of goods and services that are exchanged in markets at prices determined by market forces. The typical pattern of economic development is that at an early stage of development a large proportion of a country's economic activity is involved with primary production (agriculture, fishing, hunting, forestry, logging, and mining). As the economy grows, more income is earned in the secondary sector (manufacturing, electricity, gas and water, and construction). At a later stage of development, the economy devotes a greater proportion of its activities to providing services (the remaining five market production groups in table 1.1) rather than commodities or manufactured goods.

In keeping with this pattern, the proportion of income earned in New Zealand by primary market production is relatively small—only 8.7 per cent of GDP. This understates the importance of this sector in the New Zealand economy, however, since more than half New Zealand's exports in 1994/95 were in the form of food, beverages, crude materials, and mineral fuels. Manufacturing is the largest production group in the table, but it still produces only 18.5 per cent of income in New Zealand. The construction sector is relatively small, but it also plays a larger role in the economy than its size would suggest, since a large part of domestically produced investment is undertaken by this sector. The value added by distribution (wholesale and retail traders combined with the services of restaurants and hotels) is another very large production group of about the same size as manufacturing. The third largest group in the table is the finance, insurance, real estate, and business services group. (As a technical detail, Statistics New Zealand is forced to estimate the income earned in the banking sector, since interest receipts and payments are normally treated as a transfer of income rather than as new income, and the counterpart of this estimate is the adjustment made in the last line of the 'Market Production Groups' portion of the table, 'Bank Services Charges Not Allocated'.) The five services groups together contribute a little more than half New Zealand's GDP.

The second part of table 1.1 estimates the value of production in New Zealand's non-market sector. This is primarily concerned with the services provided by the government where the final product is not directly purchased by consumers (for example, defence, justice, public health and education, and local government). These services are valued at their total cost, and make up 10 per cent of GDP. There is also a very small component in the accounts recording the services of private non-profit organisations and the wages paid to people employed to work in households (for example, as a nanny or gardener).

The third part recognises that the price of production is increased by the addition of indirect taxes. The most important example is New Zealand's goods and services tax (GST), which is recorded separately in the table.

Adding up all these components produces New Zealand's gross domestic product, which in 1994/95 was $86,577 million. The country's mean population for that March year was 3.541 million, so per capita GDP was $24,450. This figure is taken by economists to be a guide to the average standard of living in New Zealand during that year. Note carefully that it is only a guide, since GDP does not include all forms of production, and per capita GDP does not address issues of income distribution. Nevertheless, economists argue that this statistic is a reasonable indicator both of a country's stage of economic development and of how successful its economic performance has been over time.

NEW ZEALAND'S REAL PER CAPITA
GROSS DOMESTIC PRODUCT

There are two ways in which per capita GDP can increase over time. The first is by increases in the average price of goods and services produced in the economy. This does not represent a true improvement in average living standards, but simply a drop in the value of the economy's money. Economists therefore exclude the impact of inflation from their analysis in order to concentrate on the second way per capita GDP can grow, which is by increases in the quantity of goods and services produced. The value of GDP excluding the impact of inflation on its prices is known as 'real gross domestic product'. Graph 1.1 depicts New Zealand's real per capita GDP from 1959/60 to 1997/98.

There are a couple of important points to be made about graph 1.1. First, note the upward trend. Real per capita GDP in 1959/60 was $14,758 (measured in 1994/95 prices), and by 1994/95 it had reached $24,450. This suggests that average living standards increased by about two-thirds over the thirty-five years. While this means that New Zealand is a more prosperous country now than it was a generation or two ago, it must also be noted that other developed economies have achieved significantly higher real growth rates over the same period. Following chapters will explain how dissatisfaction with New Zealand's real growth rate was one of the primary motivations for the economic reforms begun in 1984.

Second, note that although the overall trend is upwards, in some years the value of New Zealand's real per capita GDP fell. In particular, after strong growth in 1965/66, the economy slowed in 1966/67 and then contracted in 1967/68, taking two years to recover. Again, after strong growth in 1973/74,

Graph 1.1   Real per capita gross domestic product

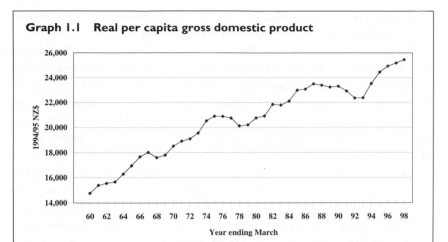

Description

To compare a country's level of economic activity over time, the impact of inflation on nominal values must be removed. This is done by Statistics New Zealand to produce New Zealand's 'real gross domestic product'. Real per capita GDP is then obtained by dividing real GDP by the mean population level of the relevant year. By excluding inflation and population growth, this statistic provides a guide to how a country's average standard of living changes over time (although note that it suffers from the same omissions mentioned in the Description of table 1.1). The graph shows New Zealand's real per capita gross domestic product for the years ending March from 1959/60 to 1997/98. The vertical axis measures this statistic using 1994/95 as the base year, so that all output is valued at 1994/95 prices.

Sources

Real gross domestic product is taken from Statistics New Zealand's INFOS series SNBA.S2AZAT, and mean population is taken from the series DPEA.SBIC.

the economy experienced almost zero growth over the next three years before contracting sharply in 1977/78. This time it took three years to recover to its former level. Similarly, after strong growth in 1984/85, the economy stagnated over the next five years, and then contracted for two years in a row (1990/91 and 1991/92) before recovering strongly in 1993/94 and 1994/95.

The reasons for these contractions (or 'recessions' as they are termed by economists) are generally well understood. In 1967 a sharp collapse in the world price of wool caused a significant fall in New Zealand's export receipts. The Wool Commission intervened in the market to buy wool at a price floor to stabilise farmers' incomes, but this was insufficient to prevent a decline in real per capita incomes. The shock fed through into the domestic economy as the loss of income in the farming community led to reduced expenditure by farmers, which in turn reduced the incomes of other sectors (a process known as the Keynesian multiplier effect).

The second recession occurred when the outbreak of the Arab–Israeli war in October 1973 cemented an accord among members of the Organisation of Petroleum Exporting Countries (OPEC) to engineer a substantial rise in the price of oil through agreed cutbacks in its supply. The impact in New Zealand was muted at first. In the June quarter of 1974, however, the Fuel Import Price Index doubled, and it had increased threefold in real terms by March 1975. At the same time, the world economy moved into a prolonged recession as a result of the oil shock. The New Zealand Government initially sought to maintain domestic economic activity at the expense of a substantial increase in overseas debt, but was forced to change this policy in the 1976/77 financial year, leading to the sharp contraction the following year.

The third recession was different in that it was the result of domestic policy rather than of overseas events. In July 1984 the Labour Party won a landslide election victory after nine years of National Party rule. In his first Budget four months later, the new Minister of Finance, Roger Douglas, announced that 'comprehensive economic and social reform would be the hallmark of the fourth Labour Government'. It was accepted that the reforms would produce low economic growth in the short term, although growth was still expected to be faster than it had been over the previous two decades. The National Party was returned to power in 1990, and in its first term of office continued the process of economic reforms on the same assumption that short-term pain would lead to long-term gain. Most of this book will be devoted to examining the reasons for and outcomes of the reforms of both governments.

New Zealand's position in the world economy

It will already be apparent that the New Zealand economy is vulnerable to changes in the global economy. This is because international trade is very important to New Zealand. Table 1.2, which analyses GDP by expenditure rather than by production, shows that in 1994/95, $17,607 million was spent on capital goods (buildings, plant and machinery, roads, and so on) and a further $1,438 million was spent on increasing inventories. Final consumption in the economy amounted to just under $65,500 million, of which 19.1 per cent took place in the public sector and 80.8 per cent took place in the private sector. More significantly for this discussion, however, 31.4 per cent of New Zealand's GDP that year ($27,173 million out of $86,577 million) was exported; similarly, the ratio of imports ($25,114 million) to GDP was 29.0 per cent.

Table 1.2   Gross domestic product by expenditure group for the year ending March 1995

	$million	$million
Government consumption	12,535	
Private consumption	52,938	
Value of physical increase in stocks	1,438	
Gross fixed capital formation	17,607	
GROSS DOMESTIC EXPENDITURE		**84,518**
Exports	27,173	
Imports	25,114	
NET EXPORTS		**2,059**
EXPENDITURE ON GROSS DOMESTIC PRODUCT		**86,577**

Description
The data in table 1.1 showed GDP analysed by categories of production. It is also possible to analyse GDP by expenditure, as recorded in table 1.2. Gross domestic expenditure is made up of four components: purchases of goods and services for consumption by central and local government, purchases of goods and services for consumption by the private sector, the change in the volume of business inventories, and gross fixed capital formation to replace worn-out capital goods and to increase the country's capital stock. Expenditure by foreigners on domestic production (exports) less New Zealand expenditure on foreign production (imports) is then added to gross domestic expenditure to give total expenditure on gross domestic product.

Source
All data in table 1.2 come from table 1.2 of *New Zealand System of National Accounts 1997*, published by Statistics New Zealand.

Because international events have such an important influence on the New Zealand economy, it is worth noting two summary statistics that provide an essential guide to New Zealand's trading environment. The first is known as the 'terms of trade', which is the average price of goods and services exported from New Zealand divided by the average price of goods and services imported into New Zealand. When the terms of trade are high, it means that New Zealand export products are worth more on world markets relative to the world price of its imports, so that the country can afford to import a greater quantity of goods and services for any given level of exports and overseas borrowing.

Graph 1.2 shows that New Zealand's terms of trade can fluctuate sharply as a result of changing world prices. The collapse of the price of wool in 1967, for example, saw the terms of trade fall by 12.8 per cent between 1966/67 and 1967/68. Between 1970/71 and 1973/74, on the other hand, large rises in world commodity prices, brought about by the combination of the El Niño weather pattern and increased demand from the Soviet Union

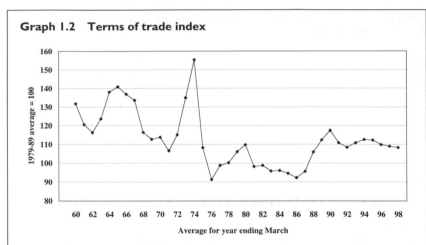

Graph 1.2   Terms of trade index

1979–89 average = 100

Average for year ending March

Description
The value of its terms of trade is very important for a small trading nation such as New Zealand. Formally, the terms of trade are the average price of exported goods and services, divided by the average price of imported goods and services. If New Zealand's terms of trade rise, it means that the prices of our exported goods have gone up faster than the prices of imported goods, increasing New Zealand's prosperity. If the terms of trade fall, however, New Zealand must export a greater quantity of exports to pay for the same quantity of imports, and domestic prosperity falls. The graph shows New Zealand's terms of trade index, using the average export and import price levels from June 1979 to June 1989 as a base.

Source
The terms of trade index is taken from Statistics New Zealand's INFOS series OTIQ.STTZZ5.

following a series of important crop failures, meant that the terms of trade rose nearly 50 per cent in just three years. A year later, after the first oil shock, the terms of trade had fallen back to their 1970/71 value. They fell a further 15 per cent in 1975/76. The fluctuations were less severe in the 1980s, but there was a welcome improvement in the second half of the decade from the trough in 1985/86. The terms of trade appear to have stabilised in the 1990s, but note that the index is still well below its value in the mid 1960s.

The second important statistic is the real rate of interest set on world markets, which determines the real return on capital that must be achieved by any new investment project in order to ensure its profitability. Graph 1.3 shows the US long-term real rate of interest to illustrate world trends. In the 1960s, it was commonplace for economists to suggest that a real rate of interest no greater than 3 per cent was the norm, as indeed the graph suggests. The first

Graph 1.3 World real interest rate

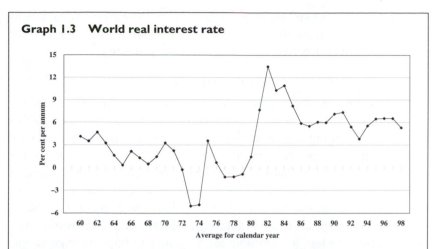

Average for calendar year

Description

The real rate of interest is defined in this graph as the nominal rate of interest less the following year's rate of inflation in the price of investment goods. This measures the rate of return that any particular investment project must achieve to be profitable. Hence, a higher real rate of interest can be expected to reduce the amount of investment undertaken by firms and so reduce a country's rate of economic growth. The graph presents an estimate of world real interest rates by showing the real rate of interest for the USA for the calendar years 1960 to 1998. The nominal interest rate used is that country's average long-term interest rate, while the inflation rate used is the percentage change in the average prices of capital goods expenditure in the USA over the next calendar year.

Sources

The long-term interest rate is taken from the INFOS series Y.USA.IRL, and the price deflator for investment goods comes from Y.USA.PIT, both based on OECD data.

oil shock in 1973 produced a substantial transfer of income and savings from oil-importing countries to members of OPEC. This situation produced real rates of interest that were generally negative in order to encourage the oil-importing countries to borrow surpluses from the OPEC countries. In other words, for several years nominal interest rates were lower than the rate of inflation generated after the oil shock. New Zealand was one of many countries that substantially increased its overseas debt at that time.

At the beginning of the 1980s, however, there were concerted efforts to reduce inflation, with central banks around the world adopting tight monetary policies. This increased real interest rates sharply and triggered a significant world recession during the transition to low inflation. Real interest rates have now fallen from their peak in 1982, but remain high by 1960s standards: graph 1.3 shows an average interest rate of 6 per cent since 1986.

This trend makes it more difficult for firms to increase their level of invest-ment, which in turn might be expected to slow down the rate of economic growth that can be achieved in New Zealand and elsewhere.

CONCLUSION

New Zealand is a small open economy. It has a well-developed manufactur-ing sector and services sector, with the latter making up more than half its gross domestic product. Non-market services provided by central and local government are a significant part of domestic activity. The level of real per capita GDP places New Zealand in the top 20 per cent of countries ranked by income, but its dependence on world trade makes the country vulnerable to changes in the global economy. In particular, New Zealand is unable to escape the consequences of a fall in its terms of trade or a rise in world inter-est rates. Nevertheless, it is possible for a country to implement economic policies to make the most of the opportunities available to it, and the remainder of this book will consider the reforms introduced in New Zealand after 1984 for this purpose, beginning with a discussion of why the policies of the 1970s and early 1980s came to be rejected as inadequate.

CHAPTER TWO

NEW ZEALAND'S ECONOMIC
PERFORMANCE, 1960–84

Chapter 1 introduced the major economic indicator of economic performance that is used for international comparisons of long-term trends: real
per capita gross domestic product. It also noted two important indicators
of New Zealand's international trading environment: the terms of trade,
and the world real rate of interest. For short-term assessments of economic
well-being, economists traditionally focus their attention on four macroeconomic indicators: the country's real economic growth rate, its rate of
inflation, its unemployment rate, and its balance of payments current
account deficit, measured as a percentage of GDP. In this chapter, time
series data for these four indicators are used to describe New Zealand's economic performance over the twenty-five years leading up to 1984. Also
shown in the graphs are comparable data for Australia. As will be discussed
both here and in chapter 3, the realisation that New Zealand was not performing as well as similar OECD countries such as Australia was an important element in the 1984 decision to initiate a programme of radical
economic reform.

THE 1960S BENCHMARK

The period under review begins in the 1960s with the New Zealand economy performing reasonably well. After the experience of the Great
Depression of the 1930s, successive New Zealand governments assumed
control over an increasingly large proportion of economic activity through
state ownership of industry and resources, and through the regulation of
what individuals and firms could and could not do. The principal objective
of this 'mixed economy' was to promote full employment by encouraging
the domestic production of a wide range of goods, regardless of whether
New Zealand had a comparative advantage in all cases. Exporters (who in

Graph 2.1 Real economic growth

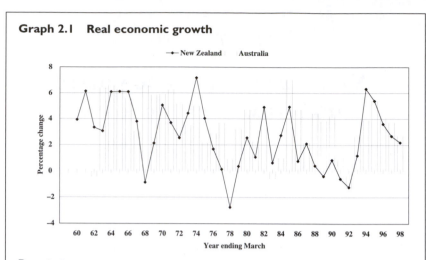

—◆— New Zealand   Australia

Year ending March

Description

Real economic growth is obtained by calculating the percentage change in a country's real gross domestic product (that is, the value of its market production excluding the impact of inflation but making no allowances for population growth). It suffers from the same weakness as real per capita GDP (see table 1.1), but measures by how much market trades grow in volume over a given time period. Also shown in the graph is a bar chart of the economic growth rates for Australia. The Australian data are for the preceding calendar year.

Sources

The New Zealand data come from Statistics New Zealand's INFOS series SNBA.S2AZAT, and the Australian data come from INFOS series Y.AUS.GDPV (based on OECD sources).

the 1960s were predominantly agricultural producers selling wool, meat, and dairy products, mainly to the UK) were obliged to sell the foreign funds they earned to the Reserve Bank at an exchange rate set by the Minister of Finance; the funds were then sold mainly to domestic producers to pay for imported raw materials. A programme of import licensing greatly restricted or prohibited the importation of various types of consumption goods, thus protecting domestic producers from international competition. Any residual unemployment that emerged under this system was absorbed into government departments such as the Railways or the Forestry Service.

At the same time, New Zealand governments attempted to promote an egalitarian society through an industrial relations system founded on strong occupation-based trade unions and a system of general wage orders designed to ensure that a man could earn a fair wage to support his family (indeed, the former Department of Statistics did not even collect data on

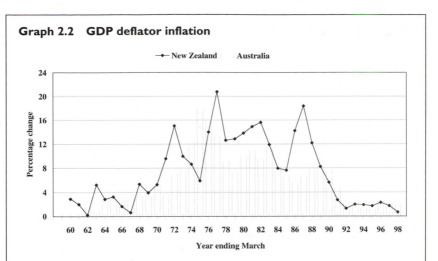

Graph 2.2   GDP deflator inflation

—◆— New Zealand   Australia

Year ending March

Description

The inflation rate shown in this graph is the percentage change in New Zealand's GDP deflator index. The GDP deflator is an estimate calculated by Statistics New Zealand of the average price level of all goods and services produced in New Zealand during any given year. Hence the percentage change in this index is a measure of the inflation generated within the domestic economy that year. Also shown is the preceding calendar year's inflation rate for Australia.

Sources

The GDP deflator index is obtained by dividing nominal GDP by real GDP and scaling to a suitable base number. The real GDP data source is the same as for graph 2.1. The nominal GDP data before 1977/78 come from the *Official New Zealand Yearbook 1992*, table 26.4, p. 453, and are linked to the current INFOS series SNBA.SB9 at 1977/78. The Australian data come from INFOS series Y.AUS.PGDP.

female wages before 1978). The government also made health, education, and social welfare universally available, funded by general taxation. Regulations were used to control the prices of many basic goods and services, such as bread, milk, telephone services, and electricity.

Graph 2.1 shows that, apart from 1967/68 and 1968/69, the New Zealand economy grew at a respectable rate of between 3 and 6 per cent during the 1960s. This was not too far out of line with other small OECD countries, but the 1967–69 recession demonstrated a serious weakness in the New Zealand economy, which was to become even more crucial in the 1970s. Its cause is well understood. In the June year of 1965/66, 30.6 per cent of New Zealand's exports by value were concentrated in just one category—wool. In the following calendar year, the world price of wool fell by more than 20 per cent, and by a further 20 per cent in 1968. The fall in demand for such an

Graph 2.3   Unemployment

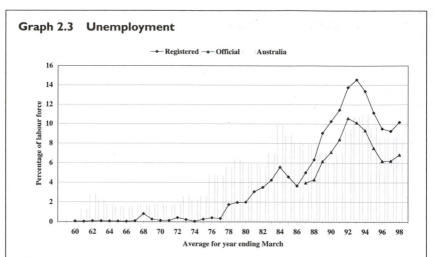

Average for year ending March

Description

The standard definition of an unemployed worker (according to the International Labor Organisation) is a person not in employment who is both available for work and actively searching for a job. The labour force is all such workers plus those in employment, and the unemployment rate is the number of unemployed workers divided by the labour force, expressed as a percentage. In New Zealand, the Household Labour Force Survey was introduced in December 1985 to produce an official unemployment rate that coincides with this international definition. Previously the unemployment rate was estimated by using the number of people registered as unemployed with the Department of Labour divided by an estimate of the labour force obtained from the Quarterly Employment Survey. The registered unemployment rate overstates the official measure, but the trends in behaviour appear similar. Also shown is the average unemployment rate of Australia for the previous calendar year.

Sources

The registered unemployment and QES employment statistics can be found in INFOS series UMPM.SD and QES.SAIZ99 respectively. The official unemployment and employment statistics come from the INFOS series HLFQ.SAB3AZ and HLFQ.SAA3AZ. The Australian unemployment rate comes from Y.AUS.UNR.

important export fed through into other sectors of the economy, and the volume of economic activity in New Zealand actually shrank in 1967/68.

Policymakers in New Zealand responded to the domestic crisis in several ways. The Wool Commission intervened in the market, buying wool into storage at a price floor to stabilise farmers' incomes (this stockpile was not disposed of until the end of 1972). In November 1967, the currency was devalued by 19.45 per cent to improve the returns to farmers and other exporters. On 18 June 1968, the Arbitration Court ruled that New Zealand could not afford any wage increase, and issued a nil general wage order (although this was changed to a 5 per cent order two months later with the support of both employers and unions). The government convened a National Development Conference, which brought together representatives of the different sector groups in August 1968 and May 1969 to improve economic planning on a national basis.

These measures were largely successful. Growth recovered in 1968/69 and 1969/70, and graph 2.3 shows that the impact of the crisis on unemployment was both small and quickly reversed. Indeed, the almost negligible rate of unemployment throughout the 1960s and the first half of the 1970s is one of the success stories of economic management in New Zealand over this period. Similarly, New Zealand's balance of payments deficit with the rest of the world, while highly variable, averaged about 2 per cent of GDP, which is considered appropriate and sustainable for a relatively small country that needs to finance the importation of large capital items (purchases of aircraft by Air New Zealand, for example).

Meanwhile, inflation generated in the New Zealand economy (graph 2.2) remained at less than 5.5 per cent throughout the 1960s, which was not excessive compared to Australia or many other small OECD countries. Internationally, inflation was not a major concern during this period, although Western nations operated under a fixed exchange rate regime overseen by the International Monetary Fund (the Bretton Woods Agreement). This system, which was anchored by the willingness of the USA to buy gold at the fixed price of US$35 per ounce, survived occasional pressures until the late 1960s, when the USA (and its allies) increased government expenditure to finance the Vietnam War, partly funded by increases in the money supply. Growing inflation in the USA was imported into New Zealand in 1968 (see graph 2.2), marking the beginning of rising inflationary pressures in New Zealand that were to persist for the next two decades.

THE COMMODITY PRICE BOOM, 1971–74

Just as the collapse of the price of wool in 1967 had triggered a sharp recession in New Zealand, large increases in world commodity prices led to an economic boom at the beginning of the 1970s. This event was brought about by a remarkable coincidence of demand-side and supply-side factors. In particular, a change in the Soviet Union's livestock feed policy made that country a much larger importer of grains at the same time as the El Niño weather effect temporarily wiped out the Peruvian anchovy crop (an important source of livestock feed), followed by other significant crop failures in 1973 and 1974. In addition the Bretton Woods Agreement came to an end in 1971, when the USA stopped its policy of converting dollars into gold at a fixed price. The world's major currencies were then free to find their own values in financial markets, releasing pent-up demand for Yen and Deutschmarks and heralding a new era of rising world inflation.

Despite the favourable impact of these events on New Zealand's terms of trade, domestic economic growth remained low by Australian standards until 1972/73. Indeed, the breakdown of the centralised wage bargaining system, after confidence in the Arbitration Court had been severely damaged by the nil general wage order in 1968, introduced a period of rising wages that fed into very high inflation rates (peaking at 15 per cent in 1971/72).

The government took a number of steps to combat rising inflation. It froze government charges; imposed a new series of wage and price controls; introduced the Farm Income Equalisation Scheme to reduce farmers' incomes (which were at very high levels during the commodity price boom); imposed ceilings on interest rates from April 1973; and increased its subsidies on woollen goods, sheep meat, sugar, and milk. It also revalued the New Zealand dollar three times during 1973 in order to reduce the inflationary pressure from import prices, but this also moved the balance of payments from surplus to a small deficit.

Inflation did fall during 1972/73 and 1973/74, but the strains imposed by anti-inflation policies on government spending, on the balance of payments, and on industrial relations meant that the economy was not well placed to cope with the UK's entry into Europe or with the first oil price shock, which were both just around the corner.

THE FIRST OIL PRICE SHOCK, 1973–77

The year 1973 marks an important watershed in New Zealand's economic history, for two reasons. First, the UK formally entered the European Economic Community on 1 January 1973, marking the end of forty years of specially negotiated access to British agricultural product markets by New Zealand exporters under the Ottawa Agreement of 1932 and wartime 'commandeer' programmes. At the time, the UK was still New Zealand's main export market despite efforts at diversification, taking the bulk of its exported lamb (72 per cent), butter (73 per cent), and cheese (66 per cent), as well as about 20 per cent of exported wool. This event therefore represented an important shift in world demand for New Zealand produce.

Second, the strengthening of the OPEC oil cartel in 1973 caused a threefold rise in the price of oil. New Zealand's heavy reliance on imported fuel meant it was seriously affected once supply contracts were renewed at the higher price. The resulting world recession, together with rapid movement towards greater

Graph 2.4 Balance of payments

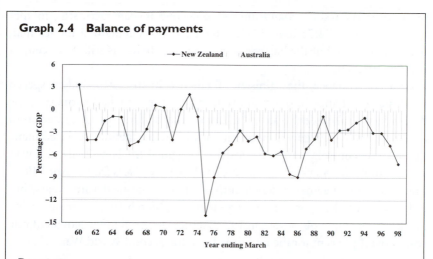

Description

The balance of payments current account surplus measures the difference between current revenue received from the rest of the world and current payments paid to the rest of the world. If the balance of payments is in deficit (as is the case in New Zealand most years), it implies that the difference must be financed by some combination of selling domestic assets to foreigners, accepting greater overseas investment in New Zealand, or borrowing on world capital markets by New Zealand residents. The vertical axis measures the surplus as a percentage of a country's gross domestic product, since it is generally accepted that a larger economy can afford a larger imbalance in its external accounts than can a smaller economy. Also shown is the average balance of payments current account surplus for Australia.

Sources

The balance of payments current account surplus comes from the INFOS series BOPA.S4AC3 (formerly BOPA.STOT169). The figure for nominal gross domestic product for years after 1977/78 can be found in INFOS series SNBA.SB9, while for earlier years table 26.4 in the *Official New Zealand Yearbook 1992* was used. The Australian balance of payments surplus comes from INFOS series Y.AUS.CBGDPR.

agricultural protectionism (especially through non-tariff barriers) in developed countries, compounded New Zealand's trading problems.

The overall impact of these events was a massive fall of 30 per cent in New Zealand's terms of trade in the twelve months to March 1975 (see graph 1.2), and the balance of payments current account balance plummeted to a deficit of 14 per cent of GDP (graph 2.4).

The government adopted the view that it needed to maintain economic growth to see New Zealand through the crisis. As later chapters will discuss, it expanded its own spending and increased its level of overseas borrowing to support domestic activity. In this objective it was successful, in that growth in the 1974/75 and 1975/76 financial years remained higher than that of Australia, but the balance of payments deficit was still 9 per cent of GDP in 1975/76.

As a consequence, the Minister of Finance in his 1976 Budget speech announced a change of direction, stating that 'the time had come for New Zealanders to take a deliberate cut in our standard of living in the interests of future solvency'. The government cut back its own expenditure, lifted many interest rate controls, removed subsidies, devalued the New Zealand dollar, and announced a 40 per cent increase in electricity prices from 1 April 1977. The balance of payments deficit improved over the next three years, but inflation reached 20 per cent in the year ending March 1977. More alarming for the government of the day, in 1977/78 the registered unemployment rate rose above 1 per cent for the first time since the Second World War.

RISING UNEMPLOYMENT AND INFLATION, 1978–84

The unemployment rate continued to rise steadily between 1978 and 1980, while inflation, in part fuelled by a second oil price shock in 1979, remained high at about 13 per cent. The government responded by developing a new economic strategy that was intended to reduce New Zealand's dependence on imported fuel; relax the balance of payments constraint on sustained economic growth; and increase employment opportunities as growth was achieved. This strategy became known as 'Think Big' because it was based on a number of large construction projects in the energy sector: in particular the Petrocorp ammonia-urea plant, the Motonui synthetic fuel plant, the expansion of the Marsden Point oil refinery, the Waitara methanol plant, the expansion of the Glenbrook steel mill, and the proposal for an aluminium smelter at Aramoana (although this last project did not proceed).

These projects were constructed in the early 1980s. Graph 2.3 records that the rate of growth in unemployment did pause in 1981/82, but otherwise this indicator continued to deteriorate until 1983/84. At the same time, the balance of payments deficit began to reverse its improving trend (in part because much of the Think Big technology and equipment was imported), and the rate of inflation continued to rise to a peak of just under 16 per cent in 1981/82. Further, the economic viability of the Think Big projects was dependent on the price of oil continuing to rise throughout the 1980s; when this did not happen (the price of oil fell in 1986), the eventual cost to the government of meeting contractual obligations to the companies involved was about $6 billion (at 1986 prices).

In the middle of 1982, the government switched its attention from unemployment to reducing the rate of inflation. For some time, it had been trying to get the Federation of Labour to agree to a wage–tax trade-off in which organised labour would accept a lower wage increase in return for tax cuts. When agreement was not forthcoming, the government decided to proceed on its own. On 22 June, Prime Minister Robert Muldoon announced a comprehensive freeze on all prices in the domestic economy, including wages, salaries, directors' fees, interest rates, and exchange rates. Initially intended to last twelve months, the freeze was later renewed until February 1984. Graph 2.2 shows that this initiative was successful in (somewhat artificially) reducing domestically produced inflation back to single figures, but unemployment climbed to 5.7 per cent in 1983/84 and the balance of payments deficit remained greater than 5 per cent of GDP.

In the 1982 Budget speech, the government announced the second half of its policy: a series of tax cuts and rationalisations that were expected to reduce income tax revenue by about 12 per cent in a full fiscal year. As the tax cuts were not funded by equivalent cuts in government expenditure, this policy also caused the government's fiscal deficit to increase (see chapter 6). The price freeze regulations, which prevented interest rates from rising, meant that the Reserve Bank was unable to control monetary expansion in the economy; credit growth therefore remained high, fuelling inflationary pressure that was artificially suppressed by the price freeze (see chapter 5).

To summarise, the incomes and prices freeze was successful in reducing measured inflation to single figures, but this was achieved at the expense of higher unemployment and a larger balance of payments deficit, while imposing considerable pressures on the government's fiscal and monetary policies. In a memorable phrase, the New Zealand Treasury argued that 'monetary, fiscal, and exchange rate policies were all given as hostages to support the freeze'. The consequences would be revealed at the 1984 general election.

CONCLUSION

The four major macroeconomic indicators presented in this chapter reveal a marked deterioration in New Zealand's economic performance after the mid 1970s, compared to the benchmark period of the 1960s. Beginning with graph 2.1, we see that real economic growth slowed for three years in a row after 1973/74, followed by a year in which real income fell by 2.7 per cent (1977/78). For the remainder of the period, a pattern of cycles of economic 'boom and bust' emerged, with reasonable growth in 1979/80 and 1981/82 being followed by negligible growth in 1980/81 and 1982/83, and then another year of moderate growth in 1983/84. Inflation, as recorded in the GDP deflator index, did not exceed 5.5 per cent throughout the 1960s (graph 2.2), but after 1970 it was never less than 5.5 per cent and often more than 10 per cent. Even the extensive price freeze at the end of the period was unable to reduce domestically produced inflation to below 7 per cent.

After negligible unemployment in the 1960s and the first half of the 1970s, the registered unemployment rate increased steadily after 1976/77 to reach 5.7 per cent in 1983/84 (graph 2.3). This became an important issue in the 1984 general election campaign, although graph 2.3 also reveals that New Zealand's rate of unemployment remained low compared to Australia's. Finally, the balance of payments deficit ballooned out to an extraordinary 14 per cent of GDP in 1974/75 after a decade of small but sustainable deficits (graph 2.4). Contractionary policy by the government initially brought the deficit back to less than 3 per cent, but this indicator deteriorated again in the early 1980s.

Throughout this period, New Zealand's economic management is most closely identified with the policies and personality of Robert Muldoon, who became Minister of Finance in February 1967 after the death of his predecessor, Harry Lake. Apart from three years in Opposition between 1972 and 1975, he retained the portfolio until 1984, and was also Prime Minister from 1975 to 1984. In this position he wielded enormous power, which he used to greatly increase the level of state intervention in the New Zealand economy. As this chapter has discussed, the results were not favourable. The electorate finally delivered its verdict in the general election of July 1984, as the next chapter will describe.

CHAPTER THREE

THE 1984 DECISION TO INITIATE ECONOMIC REFORM

Chapter 2 has described the policy responses of successive governments to the significant deterioration in New Zealand's international trading environment that occurred after the UK entered the European Economic Community in 1973, and after the two oil price shocks of the 1970s sharply increased the price of imported fuel. These policies greatly increased the role of government in the national economy, compared to the 1960s. By the early 1980s, for example, the government was determining a significant proportion of New Zealand's capital investment (in the form of the Think Big energy projects); it was subsidising certain economic activities (such as wool production and manufactured exports) while restricting others (such as long-distance road transport in competition with the Railways Corporation); and it had expanded its social welfare commitments by introducing a universal superannuation scheme for all citizens aged 60 years and older (raised to 65 years and older over ten years in a reform of the scheme announced in 1989 and confirmed in 1991). On 22 June 1982, Prime Minister and Minister of Finance Robert Muldoon announced a twelve-month freeze on all prices, wages, dividends, professional charges, directors' fees, rents, interest rates, and exchange rates, and later extended the freeze a further eight months to the end of February 1984. This represented a comprehensive and extended intervention in the most important mechanism of a modern market economy, namely the role of relative prices in allocating resources to their most efficient uses.

The government's strong economic interventions were in sharp contrast to the political strength of the ruling National Party. In the 1981 general election, National had been returned to power with forty-seven out of ninety-two seats in the House of Representatives. After appointing the Speaker of the House (who normally does not vote), Muldoon had a working majority of only one. This placed enormous strain on the government, and some important pieces of legislation, placed in jeopardy by the dissent of one or two National backbenchers, were passed only with the support of Social Credit (a two-seat minority party) or, on one occasion, with the support of a rebel backbencher from the Opposition Labour Party.

The pressure came to a head on 14 June 1984, when the government nearly lost a vote against an Opposition bill seeking to ban nuclear-powered warships from New Zealand ports, after two National backbenchers voted for the legislation. Muldoon, unwilling to tolerate the possibility of defeat in a vote on defence policy, called a snap election for 14 July, four months earlier than scheduled.

The election campaign was hard fought, with Muldoon's record of economic management becoming a central issue. In the end, the electorate delivered a landslide victory to the Labour Party, which won fifty-six seats out of ninety-five. There was scarcely time for the result to be reported in the Sunday newspapers, however, before the new government was facing its first economic challenge.

THE JULY 1984 FOREIGN EXCHANGE CRISIS

The day after the election, the Governor of the Reserve Bank of New Zealand announced that the foreign exchange market would remain closed until further notice, since the Bank's reserves of overseas currencies, and its lines of credit with overseas lenders, were almost exhausted. After two years of fixed exchange rates during the incomes and prices freeze (apart from a small adjustment in line with an Australian devaluation in March 1983), the announcement of the snap election had triggered a run on the New Zealand dollar in anticipation of a post-election devaluation. Concerned about its reserves, the Reserve Bank had immediately advised the government to devalue by 15 per cent. Muldoon had refused, instructing the Reserve Bank to support the dollar instead, principally by entering into forward contracts to buy New Zealand dollars at its current price, regardless of its value after the election. This had slowed, but not halted, the outflow, so that the Reserve Bank's reserves were very low by election day.

On the Monday after the election, the successful Labour candidates (who could not be sworn in as Members of Parliament until the official count was completed) were briefed about the extent of the crisis by Reserve Bank and Treasury officials. The meeting agreed that a 20 per cent devaluation was now required to restore confidence in the New Zealand dollar. Prime Minister-elect David Lange communicated this decision to Muldoon (constitutionally still the Prime Minister), who in a dramatic last throw of the dice refused to comply. Saner counsel in the National Party eventually prevailed, but it was not until the Wednesday after the election that the market was reopened at the lower exchange rate. Over the next three days, $1.3 billion flowed back into the country. The Reserve Bank later calculated that the cost to the taxpayer of supporting the New Zealand dollar before the election, and of meeting its contract obligations after the devaluation, was $797 million (that is, more than $1.5 billion in 1995 prices, or 2.3 per cent of GDP in 1983/84).

The new Labour Government's dramatic first week set the scene for the subsequent economic reforms, which commenced with Roger Douglas's first Budget later in the year. The experience of losing such a large sum of money as a result of attempting to defy market forces, in what was one of New Zealand's most effectively regulated markets of the time (see chapter 4), emphasised the dangers of Muldoon's style of economic management. This lesson was reinforced when the new Cabinet came to read the briefing papers of its official economic advisers in the New Zealand Treasury.

'Opening the Books'

At every general election, government departments prepare briefing papers for whoever becomes their new minister. Before 1984, these papers were kept confidential, but the Labour Government considered the messages contained in the 1984 briefings by the Treasury and the Reserve Bank to be so important that it published them both in an exercise it termed 'Opening the Books'. The title of the Treasury documents, *Economic Management*, indicated the main thrust of their argument that New Zealand's performance—one of the most lacklustre in the developed world—was a result of very poor economic management by government policymakers.

The Treasury listed five specific examples of poor economic management, the first and most important being the failure to adjust the structure of the New Zealand economy to changing external conditions. On the contrary, the government had increased its overseas debt in an unsuccessful attempt to cushion the domestic economy from the impact of falling terms of trade during the 1970s.

Second, the Treasury argued that the government had failed to deliver consistent economic policies, but had instead tended to concentrate on improving one objective at a time to the detriment of others (see chapter 2). In particular, the incomes and prices freeze had been introduced to control inflation but at the expense of other objectives such as fiscal balance, monetary discipline, and an appropriate exchange rate to prevent unsustainable deficits in the balance of payments.

Third, the Treasury claimed that the government had relied on market regulation to suppress the symptoms of New Zealand's economic malaise, rather than using more general instruments of economic management to address underlying causes. Widespread restrictions on competition in both the private and the public sectors had prevented an efficient use of the country's resources.

Fourth, the Treasury argued that domestic industry had been too insulated from the international economy by import controls, export subsidies, and the willingness of government to borrow overseas to support an over-valued exchange rate. The implication was that New Zealand had failed to concentrate its economic activity in the areas where domestic producers had a comparative advantage in world markets.

Finally, the Treasury observed that government policies had introduced further instability into the economy by expanding the Budget deficit and private sector credit in election years and contracting them again after each election. This phenomenon, known as 'a political business cycle', is clearly evident in the data of chapters 5 and 6.

THE 1984 ECONOMIC SUMMIT CONFERENCE

Armed with the Treasury's analysis of the fundamental failings of previous economic management, and with their resolve stiffened by its all too apparent consequences in the exchange rate crisis of July 1984, the new government hosted the Economic Summit Conference in September 1984. Participating in the three-day conference were representatives of the government, trade unions, employer groups, business and primary sector organisations, and social and community organisations. There were clear differences in emphasis among the various speakers, with representatives of employer groups, business, and the primary sector stressing the need for greater economic efficiency and export-led growth, while representatives of trade unions and social and community organisations called for greater social equity and more opportunities for participation by marginalised groups in society. This division was to be a constant source of tension throughout the subsequent economic reforms. Nevertheless, by the end of the third day a conference communiqué had been drafted that received the assent of all participants.

The communiqué accepted that New Zealand's poor economic performance over the previous thirty years owed much to the way the domestic economy had been managed. It agreed that sound economic management needed to pursue five basic policy objectives—sustainable economic growth, full employment, price stability, external balance, and an equitable distribution of income—while fully respecting social and cultural values and avoiding undue environmental costs. Further, it urged the government to pursue these objectives in a balanced manner, within a consistent policy framework that encompassed all the interrelated elements of the economy.

Perhaps most importantly, given the character of the reforms that actually took place, the communiqué accepted that New Zealand could no longer isolate itself from the international market place. However, it also recognised the need to protect the relatively disadvantaged from the adjustment costs of reform, and appealed for those in a relatively advantaged position to carry the greater share of restraint until the economy improved. The communiqué ended by calling on the government to continue the process of consultation initiated by the conference.

CONCLUSION

After the Economic Summit Conference, and subsequent conferences devoted to Maori economic development (October 1984) and to employment (March 1985), the government had a clear mandate to initiate a process of economic reforms. It had won a landslide election victory, following a campaign focused on economic management; the failings of previous policies had been made abundantly clear during the July 1984 exchange rate crisis; its official economic advisers had prepared a comprehensive analysis of the causes of poor economic performance in their post-election briefing papers; and the broadly representative Economic Summit Conference had unanimously agreed on the need for change.

The economic reforms began with the delivery of the first Budget of the new Minister of Finance, Roger Douglas, on 8 November 1984. He began his Budget speech by referring to the recognition by the Economic Summit Conference of the seriousness of New Zealand's economic situation, its acceptance that the economic crisis had stemmed from a failure to adjust rapidly enough to change, and its call for the pursuit of medium-term economic objectives rather than a preoccupation with the short term. He finished his speech by promising that comprehensive economic and social reform would be the hallmark of the fourth Labour Government. The remaining chapters of this book describe the policy changes that followed, and analyse the impact they had on New Zealand's key macroeconomic variables.

CHAPTER FOUR

INTERNATIONAL TRADE

Chapter 3 recorded the 1984 consensus that previous economic policies, intended to insulate the domestic economy from international market forces, had contributed to New Zealand's comparatively poor economic performance for a decade or longer. The first steps along the path of economic reform therefore involved ending a number of long-standing policies in the area of international trade and finance. These reforms can be considered under two major headings.

First, ever since an official New Zealand currency was introduced in 1934, its rate of exchange against overseas currencies had been determined by the Minister of Finance. Under this fixed exchange rate regime, the value of one New Zealand dollar measured in overseas currencies remained constant, unless the Minister of Finance announced either a revaluation (an increase in its world price) or a devaluation (a decrease). In March 1985, the government announced that in future the value of the New Zealand dollar would be determined by the interaction of supply and demand in foreign exchange markets. The reasons for this decision to float the New Zealand dollar are explained in the first section of this chapter.

Second, between 1938 and 1984 New Zealand had pursued a strategy of 'import substitution'. This strategy involved a deliberate bias in trade policies to favour the production of import substitutes (or 'importables'), particularly by restricting the ability of companies to import goods manufactured overseas. Of course, such a strategy penalises export production (by raising the cost of imported inputs above their world price). To offset this effect, the government had introduced a series of subsidies for farmers and other exporters. The result was a wide range of barriers to trade that were not only inefficient by standard economic criteria but were also often contradictory in their effects. The second

26

section of this chapter explains how these policies were reformed by the new Labour Government after 1984.

A critical indicator of the success of a country's policies regarding international markets is the level of its overseas debt. Data sources on this important indicator have been weak in New Zealand until very recently, but the third section of this chapter briefly discusses some trends evident in the data that are available.

The float of the New Zealand dollar

Graph 4.1 records the nominal and real values of the New Zealand dollar from 1959/60 to1997/98. During the 1960s, the nominal exchange rate was adjusted only once, when the Minister of Finance devalued the New Zealand dollar by 19.45 per cent in November 1967. This reduced the real exchange rate also, but only temporarily, because with domestic inflation higher than world inflation the real rate soon rose again. A 10 per cent devaluation of the US dollar meant that the New Zealand dollar effectively rose in value in early 1973, and this was reinforced by revaluations by the Minister of Finance in July and September that year on the strength of rising terms of trade (graph 1.2) and a small balance of payments surplus (graph 2.4). After the first oil shock and the record balance of payments deficit in the year ending March 1975, these revaluations were reversed in September 1974 and August 1975, but balance of payments problems persisted as the real exchange rate rose steadily throughout the second half of the 1970s as a result of high domestic inflation.

In an effort to correct the external imbalance, the government moved in June 1979 to a 'crawling peg' system, which permitted the Reserve Bank to devalue the dollar by up to 0.5 per cent per month without the Minister's involvement. This system remained in place until the incomes and prices freeze was introduced in June 1982. Over this three-year period the nominal exchange rate fell by 23 per cent, but note that the real exchange rate scarcely moved, since New Zealand's inflation rate remained significantly higher than that of its international trading partners.

During the incomes and prices freeze, the value of the New Zealand dollar was again fixed, apart from a small devaluation of 6 per cent in March 1983 when the Australian dollar was devalued by 10 per cent. In the lead-up to the 1984 election, however, demand for foreign exchange greatly outweighed its supply, as exporters and importers predicted that the government would soon be forced to devalue. As monopoly supplier of foreign exchange, the Reserve Bank was obliged to meet the excess demand by drawing down its reserves of foreign exchange. This depletion of its reserves

Graph 4.1   Exchange rate

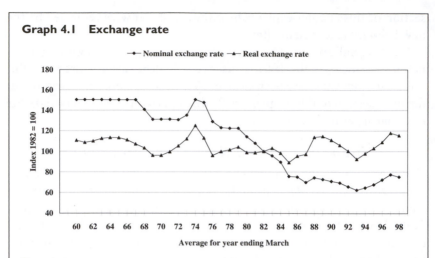

—◆— Nominal exchange rate   —▲— Real exchange rate

Average for year ending March

Description

The nominal exchange rate measures the value of foreign currencies that can be obtained by exchanging one New Zealand dollar; that is, it measures in foreign currency units the world price of a New Zealand dollar. Because there is a different exchange rate for every currency, the Reserve Bank publishes a 'trade-weighted' index based on how important each currency is in New Zealand's overseas trade. The real exchange rate is defined as the nominal exchange rate multiplied by the ratio of the price level of domestically produced goods to that of overseas produced goods. If the real exchange rate rises (appreciates or revalues), New Zealand producers lose international competitiveness; if it falls (depreciates or devalues), competitiveness is enhanced.

Sources

From 1960 to 1970, the nominal exchange rate index is a trade-weighted average of the Australian, UK, and US exchange rates published in the *Reserve Bank Bulletin*. From 1971, the Reserve Bank's official trade-weighted index is used; it can be found in the INFOS series EXRM.STW. The real exchange rate to 1980 is calculated as a trade-weighted average using relevant GDP deflator indices published in the IMF's *IFS Supplement on Price Statistics 1986*. After 1980, the real effective exchange rate index from the IMF's *International Financial Statistics* monthly publication is used.

led to the foreign exchange crisis described in the previous chapter. The 20 per cent devaluation after the 1984 election appears in graph 4.1 as the sharp drop in the nominal exchange rate for 1984/85.

The devaluation increased the price of both exports and imports in New Zealand dollar terms, and so increased the incentives for firms to plan for increased production of goods that could be exported or sold in competition with the now higher priced imports. This stimulus to the 'tradables sector' set the scene for the reforms to international trade policy discussed in the next section. However, there remained some important concerns that had not been addressed by the devaluation.

First, the lead-up to the election had shown how quickly the exchange rate could become overvalued if the Minister of Finance was unwilling to react to changes in market perceptions of its equilibrium value. Further, the subsequent crisis revealed how expensive to taxpayers such episodes could be. More generally, because the exchange rate is perhaps the most important relative price in a small trading nation such as New Zealand, the question must be asked whether its value should be set by a minister, who is subject to political pressures, or by economic competition among market participants.

Second, experience during the period of the 'crawling peg' regime had demonstrated that the beneficial impact on the tradables sector of a devaluation was likely to be quickly eliminated by rising prices. This is because imports and exportable goods are often intermediate goods or inputs to firms, so that a devaluation causes costs to rise. As firms pass on these costs in higher prices, and as workers seek higher wages and salaries to compensate, the overall result is higher domestic inflation without any permanent reduction in the real exchange rate.

Third, because of the Reserve Bank's role as residual buyer and seller of foreign exchange in a fixed exchange rate regime, policymakers were unable to use monetary policy to act against inflationary pressures. If the Reserve Bank tightened monetary policy so that domestic interest rates rose above world rates, there would be an incentive for domestic institutions to switch to world capital markets as a source of funds. When these institutions brought their borrowed funds into New Zealand, the Reserve Bank would be obliged to exchange New Zealand dollars for the overseas currency, frustrating the original attempt to constrain the money supply.

For these reasons the government concluded that the system of fixed exchange rates should end, and the New Zealand dollar was floated on 4 March 1985. A number of important steps were taken before this final decision was made. In October and November 1984, regulations restricting the ability of New Zealand individuals and companies to borrow overseas were abolished, as were restrictions on the ability of overseas-owned companies to borrow on New Zealand's capital markets. The following month a number of foreign exchange controls were relaxed, enabling banks and other suitable institutions to deal directly in overseas currencies without reference to the Reserve Bank. In January 1985 the New Zealand Futures Exchange was launched, with trade initially concentrated in contracts for the forward selling and buying of US dollars. This deregulation of the foreign exchange and foreign capital markets led to a substantial increase in foreign exchange trade, until the market was judged to be large enough for competitive forces to determine efficiently the market price of the New Zealand dollar.

Since March 1985, New Zealand has operated a 'clean float' of its currency, meaning that the Reserve Bank has not bought or sold currency in the foreign exchange market in order to influence its value directly. The Reserve Bank is not indifferent, however, to the value of the exchange rate, since if the market pushes the exchange rate down, causing a depreciation (equivalent to a devaluation) of the New Zealand dollar, this increases the price of imported goods and threatens its target of price stability. Similarly, if the New Zealand dollar appreciates (equivalent to a revaluation), imported goods will fall in price, which might lead to negative inflation.

The Reserve Bank has therefore adopted an indirect method of influencing the New Zealand dollar. If it judges that the currency is depreciating too fast (thus threatening the top end of its target inflation range), it tightens domestic monetary conditions to raise domestic interest rates (see chapter 5). This attracts a larger capital inflow from overseas, which in turn increases the demand for New Zealand dollars in the foreign exchange market and so slows the depreciation. Conversely, if the currency is appreciating too fast (thus putting the bottom end of the target inflation range under threat), the Reserve Bank loosens domestic monetary policy to reduce domestic interest rates. This decreases the capital inflow, thus reducing the demand for New Zealand dollars and slowing the appreciation.

The impact of this policy can be seen in graph 4.1. Following the float, the nominal exchange rate was reasonably stable compared to previous decades, although there is a clear pattern of steady depreciation between 1987/88 and 1992/93 followed by a steady appreciation to 1996/97. The behaviour of the real exchange rate was more erratic. It appreciated sharply in 1987/88, since the nominal exchange rate was being stabilised at a time when New Zealand's domestic inflation rate was still high compared to that of its international trading partners, beginning a period in which the competitiveness of New Zealand's tradable sector was significantly impaired. In this environment, firms in the exporting and importable industries laid off thousands of workers and sold plant and equipment where they could.

However, once the real exchange rate began to depreciate back to its long-run sustainable level in the early 1990s, old and new firms had the incentive to re-employ those resources. Indeed, by 1992/93 the real exchange rate had moved back towards its post-devaluation value of 1984/85, although inflationary pressures that emerged the following year led the Reserve Bank to tighten monetary conditions and raise the nominal and real exchange rates accordingly. The real exchange rate rose to a new peak in 1996/97, leading to complaints from farmers and manufacturers that the New Zealand dollar was significantly overvalued.

This episode illustrates an ongoing controversy in macroeconomics today. Fluctuations in the real exchange rate take time, and cause significant adjustment costs to firms in the tradables sector and to the people they employ. Further, there appears to be a distinct asymmetry in the responsiveness of New Zealand's tradable sector. When the real exchange rate appreciates, for example, businesses in manufacturing and tourism can reduce output quickly. Livestock farmers, however, typically *increase* output temporarily as they send stock to the works to generate extra cash flow and reduce the size of their flock or herd. On the depreciation side of the cycle, the first group can increase output in a few quarters, but foresters and livestock farmers (who produce a large proportion of exports) need around three years to respond.

Some New Zealand economists have argued that the failure to keep the real exchange rate at a stable competitive level indicated a weakness in the timing and sequencing of the reform programme. The continuing cyclical behaviour since 1988 depicted in graph 4.1 might also pose problems for short-run management in the future. Others, however, have argued that the sharp appreciation of the real exchange rate at the end of the 1980s and the slower appreciation in the mid 1990s constituted an unfortunate but unavoidable side-effect of breaking the devaluation–inflation cycle that had built up over the previous two decades. They claim that the reforms will produce greater stability in both the nominal and real exchange rates, as well as the domestic price level, than was possible before. Graph 4.1 might also reflect, in part, unavoidable cycles produced by the behaviour of international financial markets to which New Zealand firms will have to adapt.

TRADE LIBERALISATION

At the time of the July 1984 election, government policies on international trade involved a complicated combination of import licensing, import tariffs, subsidies for increases in non-traditional exports, subsidised access to credit, and supplementary minimum prices (deficiency payments) for agricultural production. The increase in competitiveness for the tradables sector achieved by the 20 per cent devaluation provided an opportunity for the government to dismantle most of these policies, and the late 1980s and early 1990s saw an acceleration of trade liberalisation reforms that had been initiated as early as the 1969 National Development Conference.

Import licensing was a scheme introduced in 1938 to restrict the value of imports into New Zealand at a time of severe foreign exchange shortage.

Licences, sold by the government for a nominal fee, allowed the holders to import a fixed value of particular goods in any given year. Over time, this system became an important mechanism for protecting domestic manufacturing firms, since the value of licences for goods for which there was a New Zealand-made equivalent was kept particularly low (perhaps zero). These quantitative barriers to imported goods gave rise to the term 'Fortress New Zealand', especially since economists have long understood that import quotas of this type tend to isolate domestic production from world markets and are particularly inefficient compared to tariffs.

In keeping with this theory, the first step of the new government in 1984 was to accelerate a move initiated by the previous government to a system of selling import licences by tender to the highest bidder rather than for a nominal fee. The price paid for the licences under this system provided a guide to the profits created by the import quota, and allowed the government to convert the quota into an equivalent tariff, which is more efficient. Under a tariff system, the importer pays a tax on the value of the imported goods at a rate set by the government. The size of the tariff reflects the extent of the protection being provided to domestic producers of the goods. The process of converting all quotas into tariffs was completed by the end of June 1992.

This was not the end of the reforms, however. Quotas and tariffs both have the effect of raising the domestic price of imported goods above their world price. This operates to the disadvantage of consumers but also makes it more difficult for exporters, who must pay a higher price for their inputs than do their overseas competitors. The government therefore announced in its 1984 Budget that it was giving consideration to reducing high tariff levels, and this policy was duly implemented. The average tariff in 1981 was 28 per cent, with a very high variance; in 1997, the average tariff was about 6 per cent, which is similar to other OECD countries. The 1998 Budget announced the removal of all tariffs on imported vehicles and reaffirmed the government's commitment to move towards zero tariffs by the year 2005.

Also in its 1984 Budget, the government announced that previous policies to encourage exports would be abolished. Before 1979, New Zealand had not subsidised exports to any great extent compared to import protection, although there were a host of small programmes in place to help particular segments of the exportable sector. Farmers received priority access to credit for development, for example, and there were subsidies for fertiliser and other agricultural inputs as well as special tax treatment for firms in agriculture, fishing, forestry, and tourism. In 1979 these export-oriented subsidies were raised, especially through supplementary minimum payments for certain lines of agricultural production (particularly sheep production) and export subsidies for increases in non-traditional exports (particularly manufactured goods). By 1984, sheep industry subsidies had become as high as implicit subsidies in the importable sector, a most atypical situation for New Zealand.

This situation ended with the 1984 Budget. Some of the agricultural and export subsidies were eliminated overnight, while others were phased out over a relatively short period. At the time, it was expected that the 20 per cent devaluation would cushion some of the impact this abrupt change would have on exporters, but as the previous section has discussed, domestic inflation soon offset any gain in competitiveness. The second half of the 1980s was thus a period of substantial retrenchment in the agricultural and manufacturing sectors of the economy. Household Labour Force Survey estimates suggest that between March 1987 and March 1990, 7,700 jobs were lost in agriculture (4.6 per cent) and 72,500 in manufacturing (22.1 per cent).

Graph 4.2 records the aggregate trends in the real value of exports and imports over the period 1960/61 to 1997/98. In the first half of this period, the exports of goods and services were typically less than the imports of goods and services, even before account is taken of income transfers from domestic production to the overseas owners and lenders of capital in New Zealand, thus giving rise to a persistent balance of payments deficit (see graph 2.4).

Before the reforms, many New Zealand economists argued that this feature of the New Zealand economy created an effective constraint on domestic growth, since periods of sustained growth (1963/64 to 1965/66, and 1969/70 to 1974/75, for example) were associated with sharp increases in imports and hence with a significant deterioration in the balance of payments. In the first growth phase of the business cycle after the reforms, the three years 1992/93 to 1997/98 saw the increase in imports again outpace the increase in exports, causing a significant widening of the current account deficit in 1997/98.

The trend in real exports shown in graph 4.2 is also interesting. The stalling of export growth during the world recession in the mid 1970s (exacerbated for New Zealand by the UK's entry into the European Economic Community in 1973) is very evident, and provided the impulse for early moves towards trade liberalisation before 1984. Also evident is the halt in export growth during 1988/89 and 1989/90, following the very high real exchange rate of 1987/88 to 1988/89, but a sustained improvement in export performance thereafter until the appreciating dollar again slowed export growth after 1994/95.

Graph 4.2 Exports and imports

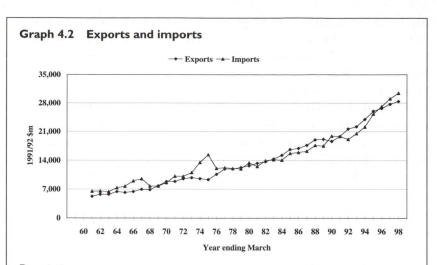

Description
The graph shows the real value of New Zealand's exports and imports of goods and services, measured at 1991/92 prices, as recorded in New Zealand's system of national accounts. Note that the New Zealand economy typically imports a greater value of goods and services than it exports, implying that it is drawing on the rest of the world's saving each year to finance its domestic aggregate expenditure.

Sources
Statistics New Zealand's modern series on the components of gross domestic product begins in 1982/83. The data for exports are found in INFOS series SNBA.S3AL and for imports in SNBA.S3AM. D. Grindell (ed.), *Consolidated National Accounts for New Zealand on an SNA Basis* (Wellington: Reserve Bank of New Zealand Discussion Paper No. 32, 1981), gives comparable data to 1978/79, and the intervening three years data were obtained by interpolating nominal data deflated by the relevant export and import price indices.

New Zealand's overseas debt

Before the liberalisation of the capital market in late 1984, there were tight controls on the ability of New Zealand individuals and firms to borrow overseas, and therefore no effort was made to record the private sector's level of overseas debt until the late 1980s. The depiction of total overseas debt in graph 4.3 must be regarded as indicative only, at least before 1993. The graph of public overseas debt held by the New Zealand Government is more reliable (subject to the note in the Description) and reveals some significant trends. Throughout the 1960s and first half of the 1970s, public overseas debt remained between 5 and 12 per cent of GDP. It then rose steadily over the next decade, peaking at just under 40 per cent of GDP in 1987. Widespread concern about whether New Zealand could sustain such

Graph 4.3   Overseas debt

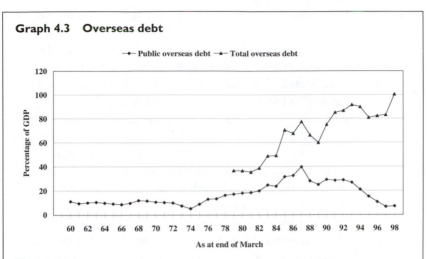

Description

Public overseas debt measures the value of the government's gross public debt denominated in foreign currencies as a percentage of GDP. This measure excludes the government's financial assets denominated in foreign currencies, and so is larger than the net public overseas debt (which is approximately zero). On the other hand, overseas residents hold a significant proportion of the government's debt denominated in New Zealand dollars, so that the level of indebtedness to overseas residents is higher than indicated in the graph. Total overseas debt is Statistics New Zealand's estimate of the aggregate gross indebtedness to overseas residents of the government, of SOEs, and of the private sector, again measured as a percentage of GDP.

Sources

The government changed the end of its fiscal year from March to June in 1990. The graph shows gross public debt held overseas at the end of the fiscal year, which is given in the INFOS series CGSA.SS up to and including 1988/89, and in CGSA.SJS thereafter. Statistics New Zealand has developed its measure of total overseas debt over a number of years, so that its current series OVDQ.SAZ9 begins in December 1992. Earlier broadly comparable data used in the graph come from OTDQ.SAZ9 (for 1989/90 to 1991/92) and from table 1 of P. Colgate and J. Stroombergen, *A Promise to Pay: New Zealand's Overseas Debt and Country Risk* (Wellington: NZIER Research Monograph 58, 1993).

high levels of overseas debt were reinforced by downgrades in the international credit rating of its public debt. The government responded by directing the proceeds of its state-owned asset sales towards debt reduction in 1988 and 1989. This reduced public overseas debt to about 28 per cent of GDP in 1990, where it stabilised until rising GDP and the achievement of operating surpluses in the government's accounts (see chapter 6) allowed further reductions to below 10 per cent of GDP in June 1997. Public foreign currency debt is now matched by public foreign currency financial assets, to keep the government's net foreign currency position at approximately zero.

Although a strictly comparable series is not available, it seems clear that the level of gross overseas debt incurred by the private sector increased substantially after the liberalisation policies of the mid 1980s. Increased overseas debt is beneficial to the borrowing nation, provided that the funds are invested in capital goods which end up having a high rate of return, or that the borrowing is matched by increased holdings of overseas financial assets. Balancing at least part of the overseas debt picture shown here is New Zealand's outward investment trend, which has also risen sharply since 1984 (official data on this are not yet available). If the overseas debt and overseas asset sides of the equation are of equal quality, then it is the net debt position that is of primary macroeconomic interest. Nevertheless, the increase in New Zealand's total overseas debt to 100 per cent of GDP in 1997/98 in a year in which economic growth was slowing (see graph 4.1) was a cause of widespread concern.

CHAPTER FIVE

MONETARY POLICY

Monetary policy is perhaps the most difficult, but also the most critical, element of contemporary macroeconomic policymaking, for several reasons. First, the quantity theory of money (one of the oldest in economics) predicts that if the money supply is permitted to grow beyond an economy's trend rate of real growth, it will only cause inflation, at least in the long run. On the other hand, if the money supply does not expand sufficiently in response to economic growth, the resulting credit squeeze can reduce investment expenditure and therefore slow capital accumulation and production capacity growth. Second, experience has shown that changes in the money supply can have a significant impact on economic activity in the short term, although the impact fades out over time. Third, a period of tight monetary policy to offset inflationary pressure will typically increase the economy's real rate of interest, which can impose significant extra costs on a government with a large stock of outstanding public debt. These considerations mean that governments are often tempted to adopt an over-expansionary monetary policy, in order to avoid any possibility of a credit crunch, to stimulate economic growth in the short term, and to avoid the interest rate implications of monetary restraint. But in the long run such a policy produces nothing but inflation.

During the 1960s and 1970s, the response of many governments was to use regulations such as interest rate controls, credit guidelines, and wage or price controls, but these became less and less effective over time. Hence, in the 1980s and 1990s the focus turned towards market methods of maintaining monetary discipline. Policies were implemented to restrict the ability of governments to use monetary policy for short-term political reasons, and to concentrate instead on the long-term benefits of maintaining some measure of price stability. This chapter will describe these trends in New Zealand's recent history, but the following section will first explain some of the banking terms used in the discussion.

A FRAMEWORK FOR DISCUSSING MONETARY POLICY

In a modern economy, most money in circulation is *credit money* created when banks and other financial institutions grant loans to their customers. As these loans are redeposited into bank accounts they increase the economy's *money supply*, which is formally defined as the value of cash held by the public outside the financial system plus the net value of the public's deposits with financial institutions. In order to understand the various policies used to control monetary growth, we first need to understand some of the key concepts involved in decisions by banks to extend credit. We can do this by analysing the items in a typical financial institution's balance sheet, which simply records its assets and liabilities in two columns. A stylised example is depicted in table 5.1.

Consider the assets on the left-hand side of the balance sheet. The first item, 'Settlement Cash', refers to the balance of a special account held by the institution at the Reserve Bank to settle its net obligations to other members of the financial system (these obligations occur every day as a result of the transactions among customers of the different institutions). The Reserve Bank does not allow a settlement account to move into overdraft, so each financial institution must make sure it has sufficient settlement cash to meet its obligations under this system. To maintain some flexibility, financial institutions also include in their portfolios a stock of 'Discountable Bills' (now called 'Reserve Bank Bills'), which the Reserve Bank promises to purchase with cash if a member of the financial system finds that its settlement cash balance is inadequate on any particular day. This facility is not expected to be used routinely, however, and financial institutions must pay a small penalty known as the 'discount rate' whenever they redeem bills early in this way. The total value of settlement cash and discountable bills is known as *primary liquidity*.

Table 5.1   Balance sheet for a typical financial institution

ASSETS	($m)	LIABILITIES	($m)
Settlement Cash	2	Deposits of Customers	750
Discountable Bills	10	Reserves and Other Liabilities	70
Till Cash	3	Shareholders' Funds	180
Government Securities	135		
Loans to Customers	720		
Buildings and Other Assets	130		
Total Assets	1,000	Total Liabilities	1,000

The third item on the assets side is 'Till Cash'; that is, the currency held by the institution to finance the day-to-day deposits and withdrawals of its customers. Also kept in reserve are other liquid assets such as 'Government Securities', which can easily be turned into cash if for any reason there is a sudden increase in the level of withdrawals by depositors. The largest asset of a typical financial institution is its portfolio of 'Loans to Customers'. The interest on these loans is, of course, the principal source of profits for the shareholders.

On the liabilities side, the largest item is the 'Deposits of Customers'. This is the component of the balance sheet that enters the definition of the money supply, since each deposit represents purchasing power for its owner. Note, however, that most deposits are created by the decision of a financial institution to extend credit to one of its customers. So, although it is the 'Deposits of Customers' component that is formally measured as money, it is increases in 'Loans to Customers' that are the major *cause* of increases in the money supply.

By definition, the value of liabilities in a balance sheet must equal the value of assets, and the residual item ensuring this in table 5.1 is 'Shareholders' Funds'. This figure represents the net worth of the institution to its owners, who carry the risks but also enjoy a share in the profits.

Because it is the interest on bank loans that generates profits for the institution, there is an obvious incentive for banks to increase credit, and so increase the money supply. There are, however, two significant constraints on this incentive.

The first constraint is that depositors are able to withdraw cash from the bank at any time. But table 5.1 shows that the value of cash and other liquid assets held by the institution is considerably less than the value of its customers' deposits. In order to maintain confidence in its soundness, and to avoid having to sell some of its loans portfolio if there is a 'run on the bank' by its depositors, the bank must maintain a prudent 'reserve asset ratio' of liquid assets to deposits. In the example shown in table 5.1, the *reserve asset ratio* is the sum of the first four assets ($150m) divided by the value of deposits ($750m); that is, 0.20 or 20 per cent.

The second constraint is that the value of shareholders' funds is very vulnerable to bad debts. Suppose, for example, that a major fall in property values caused a series of bankruptcies among the borrowers of the loans in table 5.1, who then defaulted on their debts to the value of $70m. This 10 per cent fall in the value of the institution's loans would reduce its total assets to $930m. The value of deposits would be unaffected, so shareholders' funds would be reduced to $110m, which is almost a 40 per cent fall in the value of the owners' equity. Again, to maintain confidence in the institution, the value of shareholders' funds must be sufficient to cover any such episode of serious bad debts. This ability is measured by *capital adequacy ratios*, which record the ratio of shareholders' funds to some risk-weighted measure of the bank's assets. In table 5.1, for example, a simple capital adequacy ratio is the ratio of shareholders' funds ($180m) to loans to customers ($720m); that is, 0.25 or 25 per cent.

The impact of bad debts on a country's financial system was demonstrated in a number of East Asian economies (including Thailand, South Korea, and Japan) in 1997 and 1998, contributing to the economic crisis in those countries. The extent of the bad debts forced some banks to insolvency. The closing of a bank, of course, can have a devastating impact on the savings of families or (in the East Asian crisis) on the savings of a whole generation of families. These issues are not so important in New Zealand, since almost all of its banks are subsidiaries of overseas banks. This allows the Reserve Bank of New Zealand to maintain a very light-handed approach to financial market supervision.

MONETARY POLICY BEFORE 1984

New Zealand's financial system before 1984 has often been described as one of the most regulated in the OECD. During the 1960s, the monetary authorities were able to regulate the level of credit directly; in May 1967, for example, Robert Muldoon's first mini-Budget instructed trading banks to reduce the overdraft limits of their customers by 10 per cent over the next two months. However, such regulations allowed other types of financial institution (savings banks, building societies, superannuation funds, life insurance companies, and finance companies) to increase their market share. To counter the monetary expansion produced by this phenomenon (known as *financial disintermediation*), regulations were introduced imposing minimum public sector security ratios for each of these different types of non-bank institution. The ratios were similar to the reserve asset ratios described in the previous section, except that the only reserve asset recognised was government securities. In June 1973 this system was extended to the country's trading banks, which were required to meet minimum reserve asset ratios (where the reserve assets included cash and Reserve Bank balances as well as government securities) set by the Minister of Finance. The minimum reserve asset ratios of the trading banks, and the minimum public sector security ratios for other financial institutions, could then be adjusted upwards or downwards, depending on whether the Minister wanted to tighten or loosen monetary conditions. As well as this aggregate control, the

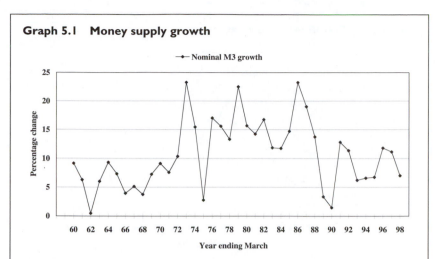

Graph 5.1   Money supply growth

— Nominal M3 growth

Percentage change (y-axis): 0 to 25

Year ending March (x-axis): 60, 62, 64, 66, 68, 70, 72, 74, 76, 78, 80, 82, 84, 86, 88, 90, 92, 94, 96, 98

Description

'Money' is any generally accepted medium of exchange. In modern economies, the medium of exchange includes banknotes and coins ('currency', issued by the Reserve Bank) plus the balances of cheque, savings, and EFT-POS accounts ('credit money', mostly created through loans by banks and other financial institutions). Credit money is by far the greater portion of the money supply. The Reserve Bank has two major definitions of the nominal money supply: M1 is termed the 'narrow money supply' (currency plus cheque and EFT-POS account deposits), while M3 is the 'broad money supply' (which also includes all other financial institution deposits). The graph shows the percentage change, or growth rate, of the latter definition.

Source

Nominal money supply data for both M1 and M3 can be found in table A1 of the *Reserve Bank Bulletin*. The growth series in the graph has been spliced to account for definition changes in 1974 and again in 1986.

Minister also had the authority to issue guidelines on how financial institutions should extend credit, and this authority was used to direct credit towards agriculture, manufactured exports, and housing.

The introduction of minimum public sector security ratios had another advantage for the government, since it created a captive market for its public debt. Further, this allowed the government to regulate interest rates tightly between 1960 and 1984 (apart from a period of relaxation between March 1976 and November 1981), not only on its own public debt but also on a wide range of financial institution deposits. This is because any fall in demand for public debt at a low interest rate could be offset by increasing the minimum reserve asset ratios of financial institutions.

The results of this method of monetary control can be seen in the graphs in this chapter. During the 1960s, the government operated a relatively

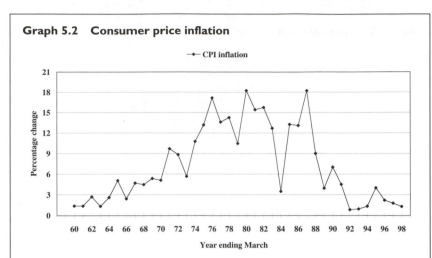

Graph 5.2   Consumer price inflation

→ CPI inflation

Year ending March

Description

The operating target used by the Reserve Bank for its monetary policy is based on changes in New Zealand's consumer price index (CPI). The CPI is a measure of the 'cost of living' of the average New Zealand household, and can also be thought of as the inverse of the real value of money (so that when the CPI increases, the domestic purchasing power of one New Zealand dollar falls).

Source

The consumer price index comes from the INFOS series CPIQ.SE9A.

small fiscal deficit of between 1 and 4 per cent of GDP each year (see graph 6.1), so that the quantity of public debt available to act as reserves for the financial system grew only moderately. This is reflected in the nominal money supply growth, which averaged close to 6 per cent between 1959/60 and 1969/70 (graph 5.1). Since real economic growth averaged 4 per cent during the period, this monetary expansion was broadly consistent with the moderate inflation experienced—about 3 per cent, as shown in graph 5.2.

At the end of the 1960s, however, a new phenomenon emerged. With strict controls on nominal interest rates, rising prices (particularly of property) meant that the real rate of interest became negative; that is, a house purchased with mortgage finance rose faster in value than the nominal interest rate on the loan. This provided a huge incentive for individuals to borrow in order to purchase property, leading to an explosion in the money supply and in the inflation rate of property. Thus, the money supply grew by 23.3 per cent in 1972/73, and urban house prices increased by more than 40 per cent the following year, producing a staggering real interest rate of negative 35.4 per cent.

Graph 5.3 Interest rate

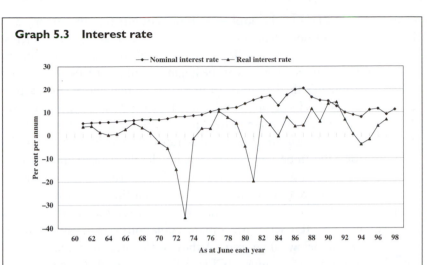

— Nominal interest rate — Real interest rate

As at June each year

Description

The nominal interest rate is the annual charge for providing a monetary loan, expressed as a percentage of the loan's dollar value. There are many different interest rates, depending on how long and for what purpose the loan is required. Interest rates in an efficient financial system are related to each other, however, with margins determined by differences in risk associated with each type of loan. Hence it is possible to single out a particular interest rate to examine trends. In the graph, the rate chosen is the average rate for new first mortgages, primarily because it is the most (although not perfectly) consistent series published for the period. Part of the nominal interest rate must compensate the lender for the impact of inflation on the real value of the loan. To account for this, the ('*ex post*') real interest rate is defined as the nominal rate less the rate of inflation over the following twelve months. The real rate above is calculated using the percentage change in the average price of urban freehold houses.

Sources

The Reserve Bank collects data on first mortgage housing interest rates, which are published after 1987 in INFOS series RBKM.SIM. Data for earlier years are provided in the *Reserve Bank Bulletin*. Quotable Value New Zealand (formerly Valuation New Zealand) collects data on open market sales of freehold houses in urban areas, and publishes a six-monthly price index for such sales in their *Urban Property Sales Statistics*. June figures were used in the calculations depicted in the graph above.

From its peak in 1972/73, monetary growth slowed following the introduction of minimum reserve asset ratios in June 1973 and the large balance of payments deficit in 1974/75, which, under the fixed exchange rate system of the time, created a drain on the trading banks' cash reserves. However, the higher fiscal deficits of the 1970s (discussed in chapter 6) increased the financial system's reserve assets faster than in the 1960s, and the money supply continued to grow at about 15 per cent. With economic growth also lower during this period, the double-digit rates of inflation that emerged in the mid 1970s are not surprising. Further, the fact that nominal interest rates did not keep pace with inflation meant that the real rate of interest again moved into negative values at the beginning of the 1980s.

The government's final attempt to preserve the regulatory approach to monetary policy was its incomes and prices freeze of June 1982 to February 1984. Not only was this designed to suppress the main symptom of loose monetary policy (inflation), but interest rates were also put back under tight controls (the impact of which can be clearly seen in the nominal interest rate series in graph 5.3), and financial institutions were asked to observe restrictive credit growth guidelines; when these guidelines failed, minimum public sector security and reserve asset ratios were raised. However, not even this set of draconian regulations could reduce money supply growth to below 10 per cent. Although the price freeze produced a recorded consumer price index (CPI) inflation rate of 3.5 per cent in 1983/84, the underlying inflationary pressures remained, to reappear as soon as the controls were lifted.

THE RESERVE BANK OF NEW ZEALAND ACT 1989

After the July 1984 general election, one of the first actions of the new government was to abolish the interest rate controls imposed as part of the incomes and prices freeze. At the end of August 1984 the credit growth guidelines were removed, to be followed by the minimum public sector security and reserve asset ratios on 7 February 1985. Deregulation gave financial institutions a sudden freedom to create credit money, and this is reflected in a renewed surge in money supply growth over the next two years (see graph 5.1). A significant portion of this new credit was used to finance speculation in the sharemarket and the property market, causing share prices to rise spectacularly until the equally spectacular crash in October 1987. Only then was the Reserve Bank able to achieve some discipline on monetary expansion and so begin the task of squeezing out the high inflation rates that had persisted for more than a decade.

Before a credible strategy for monetary disinflation could be introduced, however, policymakers needed to address aspects of previous monetary policy evident in graph 5.1. The graph shows that New Zealand's nominal money supply growth rate rose in every election year from 1963/64 to 1984/85, followed by a fall the year after the election in every case except the last (when financial market deregulation had an opposite effect). This 'political business cycle' is evidence that monetary policy was being used to engineer political advantage for the party in government rather than for the economic well-being of the country. Two things made this possible: first, under the old Reserve Bank of New Zealand Act of 1964, responsibility for setting monetary policy was given to the Minister of Finance, who could communicate changes in policy to the Governor of the Reserve Bank by private correspondence. Second, the Act provided great latitude for policy changes, since monetary policy was obliged to have regard 'to the desirability of promoting the highest level of production and trade and full employment, and of maintaining a stable internal price level'. Thus, in an election year, the Minister could instruct the Governor to relax monetary policy in order to promote production, trade, and full employment, and then the following year instruct him to tighten monetary policy in order to promote price stability.

To eliminate this temptation, the 1988 Budget speech announced that there would be a major reform of the Reserve Bank of New Zealand Act. The resulting legislation, passed with the support of both major parties in 1989, contained two critical elements for monetary policy. First, a clear distinction was made between the role of the government (which now defines the *objectives* of monetary policy) and the role of the Reserve Bank (which now designs the *policies* to pursue those objectives). Thus, it is no longer possible for a Minister of Finance to instruct the Governor of the Reserve Bank on how monetary policy should be implemented. Further, any changes in monetary policy objectives must be made public by requiring the assent of Parliament and the signature of the Governor-General. Second, the legislation defines the normal objective of monetary policy to be the single goal of 'achieving and maintaining stability in the general level of prices'. This change was justified not only on the grounds that having a single objective makes the Reserve Bank more readily accountable for the outcomes of its policies but also on the basis of economic theories such as the quantity theory of money, which suggests that the best contribution monetary policy can make to the promotion of production, trade, and full employment is to maintain price stability.

Under the new legislation, the government and the Reserve Bank are required to enter into a Policy Targets Agreement (PTA), in which a target range is set for the economy's underlying inflation rate. Until December 1996, this target range was between 0 and 2 per cent, where the midpoint was chosen to acknowledge that there is some positive measurement bias in the official statistic for inflation. Once the agreement is signed, the Reserve Bank then has the autonomy (and the responsibility) to implement monetary policy to keep inflation within the agreed range.

The post-1984 reforms also changed the framework of monetary policy, in a move away from regulatory controls towards a market-based approach. This new approach relies on the special role played by settlement cash balances in the financial system. In the discussion of table 5.1, we noted that financial institutions hold cash balances at the Reserve Bank to settle their net obligations to each other at the end of every business day and hold a stock of discountable bills to turn into cash if their cash balances are inadequate. The Reserve Bank is able to control the aggregate amounts of settlement cash and primary liquidity (that is, settlement cash plus discountable securities) available to the financial system. So if it decides to tighten monetary conditions, it can achieve this by reducing the level of settlement cash, thus forcing up short-term money market interest rates as financial institutions compete for the smaller supply. In August 1995, for example, the Reserve Bank intervened twice to reduce the supply of settlement cash from $20 million to $15 million and then to $5 million, pushing up short-term interest rates from 8.95 to 9.50 per cent. A higher short-term interest rate causes other interest rates to rise, and these in turn choke off some of the demand for bank loans that was leading to the excessive growth in credit money.

The outcome of the reforms can be seen in the graphs. Following the 1988 Budget announcement, nominal money supply growth fell sharply in 1988/89 and 1989/90. There was a rebound in the next two years, but this was to accommodate an increase in demand by the private sector for money balances following restored confidence in the New Zealand dollar, and did not threaten the Reserve Bank's disinflation target. Annual money supply growth then stabilised at between 6 and 7 per cent between 1992/93 and 1994/95, which was sufficient to finance a strong economic recovery without renewed inflationary pressure, until the last of these years.

Graph 5.3 provides a clue to the inflationary pressures that emerged in 1994/95. In June 1994 the real rate of interest turned out to be negative, since the nominal interest rate on first mortgages was 7.9 per cent and house prices increased by an average of 11.9 per cent over the next twelve months. While the nominal interest rate had risen to 11 per cent by June 1995, the property market remained buoyant, particularly for farmland and Auckland real estate, reflected in sustained credit growth that saw the broad money supply increase by more than 10 per cent in 1995/96 and 1996/97.

In the year ending March 1995, the consumer price index increased by 4 per cent. Parts of this increase were due to the impacts of one-off increased government charges (0.4 per cent), of an increase in the price of imported oil (0.3 per cent), and of increased interest rates (1.4 per cent), all of which were excluded from the Reserve Bank's definition of underlying inflation. This meant that the underlying inflation rate remained within the target range that then prevailed of 0–2 per cent (just), but there were then small breaches over the next eighteen months.

In October 1996, New Zealand held its first election under a new mixed member proportional representation format (MMP). After several weeks of negotiation, a coalition government was formed between National and New Zealand First, who held sixty-one seats out of an enlarged Parliament of 120. The first policy change of the new government was to revise the PTA signed by the Treasurer, Winston Peters, on behalf of the government and by the Governor, Don Brash, on behalf of the Reserve Bank. Reflecting widespread concern that the previous agreement had required too strong a contraction by monetary policy in response to small inflationary impulses, the new PTA widened the underlying inflation rate targets from 0–2 to 0–3 per cent. Firm monetary policy slowed money supply growth back to 7.0 per cent in 1997/98, and inflation settled around the mid-point of the new inflation target.

CHAPTER SIX

FISCAL POLICY

In June 1984, when Prime Minister Robert Muldoon announced the early election that would mark the beginning of New Zealand's economic reforms, the government's financial position was very weak. For each of the previous seven years, the public accounts had recorded a fiscal deficit above 4 per cent of GDP, causing the level of net public debt to rise from $1 billion in March 1977 to $11 billion in March 1984. Nor did this tell the whole story. Over the next two years, details emerged of further government liabilities that would add another $9 billion to the level of public debt before the end of the 1989/90 fiscal year (this was not recorded in the 1984 Budget documents because the public accounts were prepared on a cash flow rather than an accrual basis).

A decade later, this position had been turned around. By June 1994, the New Zealand Government had become the first in the world to move to generally accepted accounting practice (GAAP) for preparing its accounts; those accounts had recorded a genuine fiscal surplus, which was maintained over the next four years; and Parliament had passed the Fiscal Responsibility Act, which required the government to maintain an operating surplus on average over reasonable periods of time.

This chapter describes the fiscal policy reforms undertaken after 1984 to achieve this result. The first section presents a stylised version of the government's accounts, setting out the main categories of revenue and expenditure. The following sections then describe the series of economic reforms introduced by New Zealand's Ministers of Finance (and Treasurer after December 1996) between 1985 and 1998. The final section discusses the provisions contained in the Fiscal Responsibility Act 1994.

THE GOVERNMENT'S ACCOUNTS

Table 6.1 presents a stylised version of the government's revenue and expenditure accounts for the fiscal year ending June 1995. The left-hand column

Table 6.1 New Zealand Government Financial Statement for the year ending 30 June 1995

REVENUE	$m	$m	EXPENDITURE	$m	$m
Taxation Revenue			Transfers and Subsidies		
Personal Tax	14,857		Superannuation	4,982	
Company Tax	3,967		Unemployment Benefit	1,320	
Withholding Taxes	1,025		Domestic Purposes	1,269	
Goods and Services Tax	6,809		Student Allowances	265	
Excise Duties	1,867		Other Social Assistance	2,953	
Customs Duties	780		Other Transfers	196	
Other Taxes	908		Subsidies	163	
		30,213			11,148
Non-Tax Public Revenue			Public Services		
Fees and Fines	225		Core Administration	1,140	
Sales of Goods and Services	667		Defence	1,013	
Recoveries from ARIC	152		Economic Services	1,515	
Income from EC	65		Education	4,526	
Other Public Revenue	221		Health	4,815	
		1,330	Law and Order	1,190	
			Social Welfare	1,398	
Investment Revenue			Other	449	
Interest	778				16,046
SOE Dividends	1,204				
Dividends from EC	41		Debt-servicing Expenses		
Unrealised Gains	−65		Interest	3,757	
Other Investment Income	147		Currency Movements	−551	
		2,105			3,206
Total Revenue		**33,648**	**Total Expenditure**		**30,400**
LESS Reduced Equity in SOEs		−553	PLUS Operating Surplus		2,695
Total		**33,095**	**Total**		**33,095**

Description

The New Zealand Government Financial Statement contains a record of the Crown's revenue and expenditure during a fiscal year, using generally accepted accounting practice (GAAP). The text describes its major categories.

Sources

Estimated actual revenue and expenditure are contained in the Budget documents presented to Parliament by the Minister of Finance in June or July each year. The final version is presented in Document B1 of the *Appendices to the Journals of the House of Representatives.*

records that total revenue for the year was $33.6 billion, while the right-hand column records that total expenditure was $30.4 billion. Some of the revenue was due to a reduction in the Crown's equity in its state-owned enterprises (SOEs), so $553 million is subtracted to determine the Crown's operating surplus. This is shown as the balancing item on the right-hand side of the accounts, amounting to nearly $2.7 billion, or 3.2 per cent of GDP.

Table 6.1 presents total revenue in three categories. The first is taxation revenue, which makes up 90 per cent of government income. Nearly half the tax receipts come from personal income tax, with other substantial contributions provided by company tax and the goods and services tax (GST) imposed on domestic expenditure. Withholding taxes refer mainly to income taxes deducted at source on interest and dividend payments or on income earned by foreign residents. Excise duties are special taxes on petrol, tobacco, and alcohol, while customs duties (tariffs) are levied on imported goods.

Within the non-tax public revenue category, 'Fees and Fines' is a special heading since, like taxation, this income is derived from the sovereign power of the Crown. The other headings cover examples of non-investment operating revenue, arising from the sale of goods and services (through the policy of user-pays in certain areas of government operation), recoveries from the Accident Rehabilitation and Compensation Insurance Corporation (ARCIC, formerly the Accident Compensation Corporation or ACC), income from the Earthquake Commission (EC), and other public revenue.

The remainder of the government's revenue comes from its investments, particularly in financial assets (which earn interest to offset the interest on public debt) and its equity in SOEs (which make dividend payments to the Crown). The Earthquake Commission is also obliged to make dividend payments, and the accrual nature of the government's modern accounting system is reflected in the recognition of unrealised gains and losses on its investments (table 6.1 shows an unrealised loss of $65 million in 1994/95, arising from a revaluation downwards of the Crown's commercial forests).

Table 6.1 also presents the government's total expenditure in three categories. The first records expenditure on transfers (in which income is transferred to people receiving social assistance) and subsidies (in which certain economic activity is subsidised by the Crown). The government's largest transfer obligation is for superannuation payments to New Zealanders aged 65 years or older, amounting to just under $5 billion in 1994/95. The unemployment and domestic purposes benefits are also large items. Not all social assistance expenditure is social welfare, however; student allowances payments, for example, came to $265 million in 1994/95.

The second category presents the government's expenditure on providing public services, recorded by functional classification. The two largest functions are health ($4.8 billion) and education ($4.5 billion), with core administration, defence, economic services (including primary and industrial services, transport, and communications), law and order, and social welfare each accounting for expenditure of between $1 billion and $1.5 billion.

The final category records the government's debt-servicing expenses. Over many years, the government operated a fiscal deficit and sold public debt to meet the difference between expenditure and revenue. In 1994/95, the interest liability on this public debt amounted to $3.8 billion. Because some of the public debt is denominated in foreign currencies, a depreciation in the New Zealand dollar increases the domestic value of that debt. In 1994/95 the New Zealand dollar appreciated, thus reducing the domestic value of overseas-denominated public debt by $551 million.

THE POLITICAL BUSINESS CYCLE

The GAAP data recorded in table 6.1, which rely on accrual measures of revenue and taxation rather than on cash flows, are available on a consistent basis only since 1992/93 (the first set of Crown GAAP accounts in 1991/92 adopted a narrower coverage and have not been used in this discussion). However, the major categories are unchanged from earlier Budget tables, allowing some comparisons to be drawn over time. Graphs 6.1 and 6.2 depict trends in the government's fiscal balance and total expenditure respectively.

During the 1960s and early 1970s, the table 2 balance (the traditional measure of the difference between cash receipts and cash payments) was continuously in deficit at about 3 per cent of GDP. While this might sound high to modern ears, the deficit in those years included expenditure on investment projects that would not be included in table 6.1, which makes fiscal policy before 1974 more balanced than the figures might first suggest. Indeed, later estimates of the government's fiscal balance excluding capital revenue and expenditure (the financial balance series in graph 6.1) show that table 2 deficits of just under 3 per cent of GDP in 1972/73 and 1973/74 were associated with almost exact financial balance in both years. Graph 6.2 further shows that the government's level of total expenditure had fallen slightly from nearly a third of GDP in 1959/60 to less than 30 per cent of GDP in 1973/74, as rising shares of expenditure on education and health were offset by a decline in other areas of government expenditure.

The year 1975, however, marked a significant change in fiscal policy. During 1974, the UK's entry into the European Economic Community and the first oil shock (together with the associated world recession) began to affect the New Zealand economy. Economic growth slowed, and unemployment began to rise (see chapter 2). The government responded by increasing its expenditure in order to provide a Keynesian stimulus to aggregate

Graph 6.1   Fiscal balance

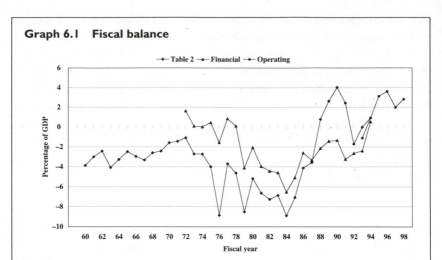

Description

Fiscal balance measures the difference between government revenue and expenditure. The traditional measure of this difference, the table 2 balance, recorded revenue and expenditure on a cash flow balance. This measure produced a fiscal surplus in 1987/88 by including revenue from the sale of state assets. To correct for this, Treasury officials introduced a better measure known as the 'adjusted financial balance', which excluded revenue from asset sales (including forestry cutting rights). Under the Public Finance Act of 1989, the government moved to an accrual basis for recording revenue and expenditure flows, using generally accepted accounting principles (GAAP). The measure of fiscal balance produced by this method is called the 'operating balance', and it has replaced both previous measures in line with the strict requirement to use GAAP laid down by the Fiscal Responsibility Act of 1994. Note that the government's fiscal year changed from the year ending March to the year ending June in 1989/90.

Sources

Table 2 data and operating surplus data all come from the government's Budget documents. Financial balance data for 1984/85 to 1993/94 also come from Budget documents, but earlier figures are derived from the table 2 deficit using the estimates of 'Lending Minus Repayments' published by David Webber in *Tracking Down the Deficit*, New Zealand Planning Council EMG Report No. 8, May 1987.

demand. Graph 6.2 shows that within two years total expenditure had jumped to nearly 40 per cent of GDP and that, apart from a brief period of restraint in 1976/77 following the change of government in November 1975, expenditure remained at about that level until 1984/85.

The pattern in the table 2 balance of graph 6.1 is equally pronounced. In 1974/75 the deficit had increased to 4 per cent of GDP and to 8.9 per cent in 1975/76. Note, however, that the financial deficit remained relatively small

Graph 6.2 Government expenditure

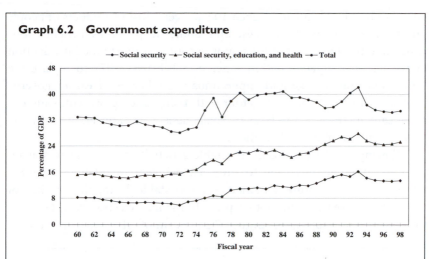

—•— Social security —▲— Social security, education, and health —•— Total

Description

The top series in graph 6.2 shows total government expenditure. The data depict table 2 cash flow definitions from 1959/60 to 1991/92 and operating balance GAAP definitions from 1992/93 to 1997/98. Note that the change in definitions added approximately $2 billion to both revenue and expenditure in 1992/93, so that the increase shown that year was not due to any policy expansion (instead, the table 2 definitions recorded a fall in total expenditure to less than 39 per cent of GDP). Since the late 1970s, more than half of government expenditure has occurred on just three items: social security, education, and health. The bottom series in graph 6.2 records spending on social security, while the gap between the bottom two series records education and health expenditure.

Sources

Total government expenditure data come from Budget documents. Social security, education, and health data also come from Budget documents, with some adjustment to the data before 1969/70 to ensure consistency with changes in definition introduced in the 1970 Budget.

at only 1.6 per cent, indicating that most of the increased expenditure that year was on investment projects rather than on increased transfer payments or consumption expenditure. After the change of government in 1975, the new Prime Minister and Minister of Finance, Robert Muldoon, reduced the table 2 deficit to less than 4 per cent of GDP. This restraint turned out to be temporary. By the next election in 1978/79, the deficit was back at 8.5 per cent, but this time the financial balance was also in significant deficit at 4.1 per cent of GDP.

The explanation can be found in graph 6.2. In 1972/73, spending on social security (including social welfare benefits) had been 6.9 per cent of

GDP, but by 1978/79 it had reached 10.9 per cent. Rising numbers of people on the unemployment, widows, and domestic purposes benefits contributed to this increase, but the major portion was due to the introduction of the national superannuation scheme in February 1977 to replace the more parsimonious age and superannuation schemes of earlier governments. This policy change, together with rising unemployment, caused a significant increase in the level of social assistance transfers paid by the government out of general taxation.

Following the 1978 election, the table 2 deficit (graph 6.1) was again reduced, although this time to only 5.2 per cent of GDP in 1979/80. Government expenditure remained relatively stable during the first half of the 1980s, but revenue did not keep up. In the next election year, 1981/82, the deficit again peaked, this time at 7.3 per cent of GDP. Further, the 1982

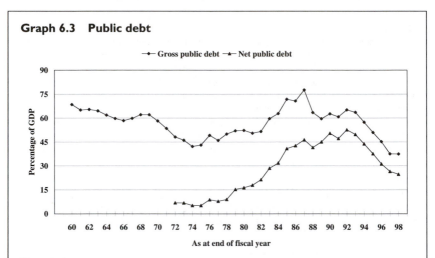

Graph 6.3 Public debt

Description
Gross public debt records the total value of the government's overseas and domestic debt, measured as a percentage of GDP. Before the end of the 1970s, almost all of the debt incurred was borrowed on behalf of the government's trading departments (such as Energy, Works, and Railways), and so was matched by financial assets backed by the investment projects of these departments. Net public debt records the value of the government's debt less the value of its offsetting financial assets. Net public debt is a better measure of the liability of taxpayers to the owners of public debt.

Sources
Gross public debt data can be found in the INFOS series CGSA.SJR (after 1989/90) and CGSA.SR (for earlier years). Net public debt data are provided in Budget documents after 1989/90, and for earlier years were provided by the New Zealand Debt Management Office.

Budget announced tax cuts that were not matched by any reductions in government expenditure, so that by 1983/84 the table 2 deficit was back to 8.9 per cent of GDP, and, more alarmingly, the financial deficit had reached 6.5 per cent of GDP.

This was the fiscal position inherited by the new government after the election of July 1984. Compared to the healthy situation of a decade before, the public accounts revealed a severe gap between expenditure and income, produced by large increases in transfer payments and reduced tax receipts (in real terms) rather than by increased investment in public infrastructure. Further, the data reveal a clear political business cycle in which fiscal policy was strongly expansionary in election years and then contractionary in post-election years, introducing an unnecessary degree of uncertainty and variability into the New Zealand economy.

The overall trend of that cycle was for the Budget deficit to increase over time. This produced an unsustainable growth in the level of net public debt (see graph 6.3), which had been about 5 per cent of GDP in March 1974, reached 31.8 per cent in March 1984, and would climb to 40.8 per cent by March 1985 (partly as a result of the impact of the July 1984 devaluation on the domestic value of overseas-denominated debt). Correcting these imbalances became an urgent priority for successive governments over the next ten years.

FISCAL REFORM 1984–87

The process of fiscal policy reform began with the first Budget of the new government, presented by Roger Douglas to Parliament on 8 November 1984, less than four months after the election. The Budget speech announced radical changes in three major areas.

First, the government announced that it would progressively eliminate subsidies to agricultural producers, exporters of manufactured goods, and the state-owned suppliers of electricity and coal. This reform had the beneficial effect of reducing government expenditure (and hence the fiscal deficit), but its primary purpose was to improve economic efficiency by allowing unsubsidised market prices to send proper signals to producers and consumers about the actual costs and the true state of demand for inputs and outputs. The agriculture sector was particularly hard hit by this policy change, since subsidies such as the supplementary minimum prices for meat, wool, and milkfat production had been imputed into higher land values. The removal of subsidies saw the price of farms return to their pre-subsidy levels, causing large capital losses to farmers. The resulting loss of equity relative to debts meant that some farmers were obliged to sell their farms, while others survived only by family members earning extra income through non-farm work or by ruthlessly cutting back expenditure on items such as fertiliser and capital equipment (thus spreading the distress to small rural towns and cities in a classic example of the Keynesian multiplier in operation).

Second, the government announced a fundamental reform of the tax system that would remove some tax exemptions; make certain fringe benefits taxable; lower marginal income tax rates; and introduce a comprehensive goods and services tax (GST) on domestic expenditure. The overall objective was to broaden the tax base (by removing certain exemptions and by taxing expenditure as well as incomes), so that a lower tax rate could be used to collect the same amount of revenue. This in turn would increase the incentives to earn extra income and thus increase work effort. The details were released in a special statement on 20 August 1985, and were implemented on 1 October 1986. Income tax rates were reduced from 20 to 15 per cent at the bottom end of the income scale and from 66 to 48 per cent at the top end, while the new goods and services tax rate was set at 10 per cent on all domestic expenditure (except financial services), replacing the previous system of sales taxes of between 10 and 50 per cent on certain selected goods.

Third, the government sought to protect low-income households in a number of ways. It introduced two new programmes to provide targeted assistance to low- and middle-income families: Family Support and Guaranteed Minimum Family Income. Although the link was not explicitly made, this extra assistance was partially funded by a controversial tax surcharge on high-income earners receiving national superannuation. The government also increased all benefits by 5 per cent on the same day that GST was introduced (since the net effect of the new tax and the ending of the old sales taxes was expected to increase prices by about 5 per cent). Finally, a commitment was made that during its first term the government would protect key areas of the welfare state (particularly education, health, housing, and income assistance) from the major thrust of the fiscal reforms.

The overall impact of the Budget reforms can be seen in graphs 6.1 and 6.2. Government expenditure began to fall as a percentage of GDP after its peak of 40.9 per cent in 1983/84, while expenditure on social security, education, and health remained comparatively stable at about 22 per cent of GDP. The table 2 fiscal deficit (table 6.1) also began to close, reduced from 8.9 per cent of GDP in 1983/84 to 3.6 per cent in 1986/87.

In the 1987 Budget, just before that year's general election, Roger Douglas made a startling announcement: New Zealand had achieved its first fiscal surplus in thirty-five years. This was partly due to the success of the tax reforms in increasing tax revenue, and partly due to a change in the operating principles of former government trading departments, requiring the SOEs that replaced them to pay dividends to the government (see chapter 7). Most importantly, however, the surplus was due to the government's decision to sell shares in a number of its businesses. Because the table 2 deficit was still calculated on a cash flow basis, the revenue from these sales was included in the public accounts, thus producing the fiscal surplus.

The government recognised that the revenue from selling public assets should not be treated in the same way as revenue from taxation and current operations. Hence the Treasury introduced the concept of the government's financial balance, defined as the table 2 balance less the net revenue from asset sales and purchases. The New Zealand Planning Council later provided backdated estimates of this measure to the 1971/72 fiscal year (see the notes on sources in graph 6.1). The financial balance showed some improvement in 1987/88 but not to the extent indicated by the table 2 balance.

THE 1987 SHAREMARKET CRASH

In the event, a table 2 surplus was achieved as expected, but the 1987/88 fiscal year was more notable for a serious division within the government over the pace and direction of economic reforms after the sharemarket crash of October 1987. At the end of March 1985, the Barclays Share Price Index for the value of the New Zealand sharemarket had been 1463. Twelve months later, the index had increased by more than 50 per cent to 2293 and by a further 42.5 per cent by the end of March 1987. The index peaked at 3969 on 18 September 1987 and was still at 3430 one month later on 19 October. The next day, however, the index fell by 14.7 per cent to 2925. It continued to slide for the rest of the year, settling at 1942 on 31 December, less than half its peak value three and a half months earlier.

The Labour Party had been returned to power with an increased majority in the general election of August 1987, and Finance Minister Roger Douglas argued from this that the government had a mandate to increase the pace of economic reform as the best policy response to the sharemarket crash. Consequently, he and his Cabinet colleagues announced on 17 December 1987 that the government intended in the following year to introduce a single rate of income tax (later set at 24 cents in the dollar); to increase GST to 12.5 per cent; to begin a five-step plan to significantly reduce tariff rates; to lower the level of import barriers protecting the motor vehicle industry; to deregulate the telecommunications industry; and to undertake a comprehensive reform of local and regional government. In the New Year, however,

Prime Minister David Lange announced that the flat tax proposal would not proceed, making the famous comment that it was time to stop for a cup of tea in the economic reform process. (A compromise later moderated the income tax cuts to 33 cents in the dollar at the top end of the income scale, introduced from 1 October 1988.)

The Prime Minister's announcement was made without prior discussion with his Finance Minister, and much of 1988 was taken up by public conflict between the two men. As graph 4.1 shows, this year proved to be one of the key turning points in the real exchange rate cycle, perhaps reflecting the government's loss of economic direction. At the end of the year Douglas resigned as Minister of Finance and was replaced by David Caygill. On 7 August 1989 David Lange also resigned, to be succeeded by Geoffrey Palmer.

Apart from the flat tax proposal, Caygill continued the programme of economic reforms outlined in the December 1987 package. GST was increased to 12.5 per cent from 1 July 1989, and the government continued to make progress on reducing its expenditure as a proportion of GDP; by 1989/90, the ratio had fallen to 36.0 per cent. The financial deficit also narrowed, and by 1989/90 it had been reduced to 1.3 per cent of GDP, its lowest level for more than a decade. The public asset sales programme continued: over a four-year period from 1988 to 1991, the government privatised New Zealand Steel, Petrocorp, the Development Finance Corporation (DFC), Post Bank, Air New Zealand, the Rural Bank, State Insurance, the long-term cutting rights to certain state forests, Housing Corporation mortgages, and Telecom (at $4.25 billion the largest of the asset sales, in September 1990), as well as a number of smaller business operations. The revenue from these sales was used to stabilise gross public debt at about 60 per cent of GDP (graph 6.3), although ongoing financial deficits saw net public debt continue to rise to 50.5 per cent of GDP in June 1990.

THE 1990 FISCAL CRISIS

The October 1990 general election produced a landslide victory for the National Party. The incoming government was then advised by Treasury that the fiscal position had deteriorated sharply since the Budget speech in July, in which Caygill had announced a financial surplus for the 1990/91 fiscal year. However, this surplus had been produced by not fully costing all of the policy changes announced in the Budget, and by treating the sale of long-term forestry cutting rights as current revenue (using a technical loophole in international definitions, which assume that forestry cutting rights are short-term only; the financial balance data in graph 6.1 have been adjusted to exclude this item). Further, the recession that began in 1990, accompanied by very high interest rates as the Reserve Bank worked to contain rising inflationary pressures, reduced tax revenue and imposed extra costs on the government (such as higher welfare transfer payments and higher interest charges on its public debt). Thus the actual result for the 1990/91 financial balance was not a surplus but a deficit of 3.2 per cent of GDP, and the Treasury's post-election briefing projected that it could rise to 6.3 per cent by 1993/94 if policies did not change.

The new Minister of Finance, Ruth Richardson, revealed the extent of the fiscal crisis on 5 November. A special statement issued on 19 December explained how the government intended to address the problem, principally by cutting back income support entitlements to most categories of social welfare beneficiaries by between 2.9 and 24.7 per cent from 1 April 1991, and by setting up a series of reviews to reduce expenditure in other areas. The benefit cuts caused considerable poverty among beneficiaries, reflected in a large surge in demand for assistance from private charities such as foodbanks. The cuts were anticipated to generate savings in social welfare transfer payments of $1.275 billion, or about 1.7 per cent of GDP, in their first fiscal year (1991/92), but graph 6.2 shows that expenditure on social security continued to increase as a percentage of GDP, since the deepening recession caused GDP to fall and the number of people relying on unemployment benefits to rise. Once the economy returned to strong growth in 1993/94 and 1994/95, however, social welfare payments fell and tax revenues increased, so that a small but genuine financial surplus was achieved in 1993/94, increasing to an operating surplus of 3.6 per cent of GDP in 1994/95.

After the National Government was returned to power in the general election of 1993 by a very slim majority, Prime Minister Jim Bolger dismissed Ruth Richardson as Minister of Finance (which marked another turning point in the real exchange rate; see graph 4.1). Thus it fell to her replacement, Bill Birch, to determine the government's response to the rising surpluses forecast for beyond the 1994/95 fiscal year. His first priority was to retire public debt, until net public debt was below 30 per cent of GDP in the short term and about 20 per cent in the long term. Birch's second priority, once the short-term goal had been achieved, was to introduce a programme of tax cuts to boost the disposable incomes of New Zealanders and to enhance New Zealand's international competitiveness. This programme was announced in February 1996, and was based on reducing New Zealand's middle income tax rate in two stages (from 24 to 21.5 per cent in July 1996 and to 19.5 per cent in July 1996). The government also introduced a small

Independent Family Tax Credit, available only to families not receiving income support from a social security or accident compensation source. Each of the programme's two stages was forecast to involve approximately $1.3 billion, and so represented a significant boost to aggregate demand.

These priorities of lower debt and lower taxes were the subject of considerable debate, as other political parties argued that more of the surplus should be spent on the core government areas of social security, education, and health. This debate is often expressed as a question of the appropriate size of government, with supporters of tax cuts arguing in favour of a smaller public sector and supporters of increased expenditure arguing for a larger public sector. In such a discussion, it is important to distinguish between the government's role in redistributing resources (through transfer payments) and its role in consuming resources (including the labour resources of its employees).

Graph 6.4 depicts time series for the levels of private sector real consumption and public sector real consumption, expressed in millions of 1991/92 dollars. Of the two series, public consumption appears as the more stable, but in fact there are three distinct periods in this series. Between 1960/61 and 1981/82, real public consumption grew at the rate of about 3.5 per cent per annum; it then slowed but remained positive at about 1 per cent per annum between 1981/82 and 1992/93. This illustrates how difficult it is for public consumption expenditure to be reduced, even by a government intent on fiscal restraint, compared to the ease with which subsidies and transfers can be withdrawn or scaled down. It was only in 1993/94 and 1994/95, ten years after the reform programme began, that public consumption began to decline (temporarily) in real terms.

In contrast, private real consumption also grew by about 3.5 per cent per annum in the first half of the period under review, but only until 1975/76. During the late 1970s, the ratio of public to private consumption increased from 25 per cent to 30 per cent in 1981/82. Private consumption growth recovered in the mid 1980s, but fell again in the 1990/91 and 1991/92 recession. Strong growth in private sector consumption in 1993/94 and 1994/95, at a time when public sector consumption was falling, has brought the ratio of public to private consumption back to its earlier value of about 25 per cent.

THE COALITION GOVERNMENT

On 12 October 1996, New Zealand held its first election under the electoral system of MMP. After nearly two months of negotiations with National and Labour, New Zealand First entered into a coalition government with National, with the respective leaders signing a Coalition Agreement on

Graph 6.4   Consumption

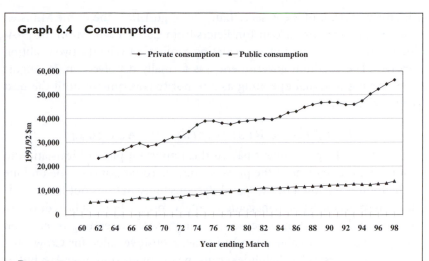

→ Private consumption → Public consumption

Year ending March

Description
The graph shows the real value of New Zealand's consumption expenditure by the private sector and by the public sector (central and local government).

Sources
Statistics New Zealand's modern series on the components of GDP begins in 1982/83. The data for real private consumption and real public consumption are found in INFOS series SNBA.S3AG and SNBA.S3AF respectively. D. Grindell (ed.), *Consolidated National Accounts for New Zealand on an SNA Basis* (Wellington: Reserve Bank of New Zealand Discussion Paper No.32, 1981), gives comparable data to 1978/79, and the intervening three years' data were obtained by intrapolating nominal data deflated by the consumer price index.

10 December 1996. The Agreement postponed the second round of the 1996 tax reduction programme from 1 July 1997 to 1 July 1998 in order to allow for an extra $5 billion to be spent over the three years to 1999/2000. This included abolishing the tax surcharge on high-income superannuation recipients from 1 April 1998. This policy was based on economic projections of average GDP growth of 3.4 per cent per annum. In fact this growth rate was not achieved (see chapter 9), and indeed the signing of the Coalition Agreement appears to mark the beginning of the latest cycle in the real exchange rate of graph 4.1. Consequently, the government reduced its planned expenditure in order to avoid moving into an operating deficit.

The Coalition Agreement also introduced a new position of Treasurer in Cabinet, initially held by the leader of the New Zealand First party, Winston Peters. This position was made the senior position of the finance portfolio, so that the Treasurer has the principal responsibility of preparing the government's annual budget and of negotiating the Policy Targets Agreement with the Governor of the Reserve Bank. In August 1998 the Prime Minister, Jenny Shipley, dismissed Winston Peters from Cabinet (and from the position of Treasurer) as part of an escalating conflict between the two coalition partners. The coalition government was formally dissolved on 26 August 1998, leaving National operating as a minority government until the next general election.

THE FISCAL RESPONSIBILITY ACT 1994

In June 1994, the government passed this important piece of legislation to ensure that the reforms of the previous decade could not easily be undone in the future. Section 4 of the Fiscal Responsibility Act sets out five principles of responsible fiscal management: total Crown debt must be reduced to prudent levels; operating expenses must not exceed operating revenue on average, over a reasonable period of time; a positive value for Crown net worth (that is, assets less liabilities) must be maintained to provide a buffer against adverse shocks; fiscal risks must be managed prudently; and the level and stability of tax rates should be reasonably predictable for future years. The Act does not prescribe exactly what a prudent level of total Crown debt is, but the government has indicated that the standard it has adopted is net public debt in the range of 20–30 per cent of GDP.

The Act then sets out a precise cycle of financial reporting, beginning with a Budget Policy Statement before 31 March each year specifying the government's long-term objectives and short-term strategies for fiscal policy, and explaining how these are consistent with the principles of responsible fiscal management contained in section 4 of the Act. The Budget speech in June or July must be accompanied by an Economic and Fiscal Update providing Treasury forecasts for the next three years, and by a Fiscal Strategy Report explaining how the Budget is consistent with the Budget Policy Statement and projecting trends in the key fiscal variables to show whether they are consistent with the long-term objectives. Finally, in December each year or before a general election, the Treasury must publish another Economic and Fiscal Update.

The strict standards it sets for these financial reports are a significant part of the Act. In particular, all the Crown's financial reports must use generally accepted accounting practice (section 5) and must disclose any policy decisions or other matters that may affect the future fiscal situation (section 11). Thus it is no longer legal for the government to use cash-based accounting to conceal liabilities entered into, or to hide any deterioration in the fiscal accounts during the lead-up to an election. Statements that these requirements have been observed must be signed by the Minister of Finance and the Secretary of the Treasury at the beginning of every Economic and Fiscal Update.

This Act, the first of its type in the world, has introduced a degree of integrity and transparency into New Zealand's public accounts that is rare in other countries.

CHAPTER SEVEN

INDUSTRY POLICY

The most important source of sustained improvement in a country's average standard of living is growth in the productivity of its employed labour force. The greater the value of goods and services produced per worker employed (or per hour worked), everything else being equal, the greater the material prosperity of the population.

Graph 7.1 presents a measure of New Zealand's labour productivity, defined as the value of real GDP (excluding agriculture, to be consistent with employment statistics) divided by the number of full-time equivalent jobs as measured by the Quarterly Employment Survey (which excludes the agriculture sector). The series shows that between 1959/60 and 1973/74, labour productivity grew steadily, averaging 1.3 per cent per annum over these fourteen years. This rate was relatively low by international standards, but worse was to come in the decade after the first oil shock. Productivity growth stalled in 1974/75 and 1975/76, and then fell for each of the last three years of the decade. Two years later, New Zealand's labour productivity in 1980/81 was still 1.9 per cent lower than it had been in 1973/74. There was a strong improvement in 1981/82, and again in 1983/84, but even allowing for these gains, labour productivity growth over the ten years from 1973/74 to 1983/84 averaged a dismal 0.6 per cent per annum.

The slowdown in productivity growth in the mid 1970s was experienced by all Western countries, but not to the same extent nor for as long as in New Zealand. The situation led policymakers after 1984 to design some far-reaching reforms intended to improve the productivity performance of New Zealand's producer organisations in both the public and private sectors. These changes are described in this chapter under four headings: the first describes the reform of government producer organisations; the second explains how promoting competition was an objective used to guide industry

Graph 7.1 Labour productivity

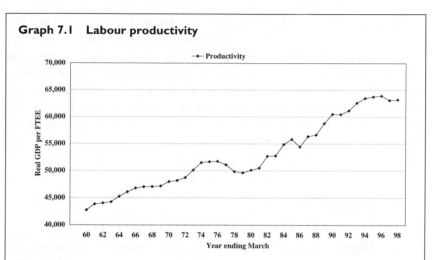

Description

Labour productivity measures the average amount of output produced by each worker employed. Formally, it is the value of real gross domestic product divided by the number of full-time equivalent employees (FTEE). The data used to produce the above graph exclude the agriculture sector from both the output and the employment figures.

Sources

Real GDP data come from INFOS series SNBA.SZ999. Real output in the agriculture series (which is subtracted from real GDP) comes from SNBA.SX1AA after 1977/78 and for earlier years is derived from data in various editions of the *New Zealand Official Yearbook.* Full-time equivalent employment is defined as the number of full-time jobs plus half the number of part-time jobs. Full-time employment and part-time employment come from QESQ.SAIZ91 and QESQ.SAIZ92 respectively, after 1987/88. For earlier years, data from the Department of Labour's Quarterly Employment Survey were used, published in table 1 of *Employment Statistics, 1979–1983* and in various issues of the *New Zealand Official Yearbook,* the *Monthly Abstract of Statistics* and *Key Statistics.* The QES data do not include the agriculture sector in their coverage.

policy generally; the third summarises the transitional and enduring impact of the reforms on productivity and on its two elements, output and employment growth; and the final section considers one of the important elements in labour productivity growth, namely investment in physical capital.

THE REFORM OF GOVERNMENT PRODUCER ORGANISATIONS

A feature of New Zealand's industrial structure in 1984 was the prevalence of government organisations in industries as diverse as banking, insurance, legal services, superannuation services, railways, air travel, bus travel, shipping, engineering and construction, architectural services, port and airport services, electricity and gas, telecommunications, primary produce marketing, coal-mining, forestry, oil refining, steel production, printing, broadcasting, hotel accommodation, computing services, postal services, and weather forecasting. In some industries, the relevant government organisation operated as a statutory monopoly, while in others it controlled a large proportion of output and was a significant employer in the industry. In all cases, policy advisers in the Treasury were concerned that the managers of these producer organisations lacked proper incentives to use resources efficiently, for a number of reasons.

First, it was difficult to assess managerial performance in the public sector, since managers were typically required to pursue a mixture of commercial and social objectives. The New Zealand Forestry Service, for example, was obliged to manage state forest resources commercially, but was also required to provide for conservation, recreation, and scientific uses, and was frequently directed to play a role in absorbing rising unemployment in certain districts. As the trade-offs between commercial and non-commercial objectives were not made explicit, it was impossible to judge whether either set was being efficiently pursued.

Second, compared to private sector managers, managers in government organisations faced weak sanctions for poor performance. If a private sector company performs below market expectations, this is immediately reflected in a reduction in the value of its shares, making the company vulnerable to a take-over by more efficient managers. This discipline is not present in a public organisation, nor could it be simulated without clarifying managerial responsibilities and objectives.

Third, managers in government organisations generally faced political constraints and advantages not experienced by private sector managers. Funding for capital investment, for example, took place through the annual Budget round of Parliament rather than through normal banking or equity processes. This not only made long-term planning impossible; it also meant that managers did not face the normal market disciplines associated with capital finance (the obligation to earn a market rate of return on invested capital, for example).

Fourth, it was clear that some government organisations were not charging the true opportunity cost of their services, either because their accounting systems had not been designed to measure economic costs appropriately or because the price of the service had become a political issue rather than a commercial decision. A good example is the price of electricity, which many argued was kept artificially low for political reasons, whereas a higher price would have better reflected the long-term cost of constructing extra generating capacity and encouraged greater energy efficiency by consumers.

Fifth, the effect of subsidised finance and regulated below-cost pricing was to give some government organisations an unfair advantage over their competitors. In some cases, this advantage was reinforced by legislation that placed restrictions on the entry of private sector competitors into the industry. These arrangements ensured that government organisations could maintain market share without needing to have regard to productivity performance.

In December 1985, the government announced a new framework for state-owned enterprises (SOEs), based on the following five principles: responsibility for non-commercial functions would be separated from SOEs; the principal responsibility of managers would be to run the SOEs as successful business enterprises; managers would be given the power to make decisions on how to meet agreed performance objectives so that they could be held accountable; unnecessary barriers to competition would be removed; and individual SOEs would be reconstituted under the guidance of boards of directors, generally appointed from the private sector.

Twelve months later, these principles were given legislative effect in the State Owned Enterprises Act 1986. Section 4 of the Act states:

> the principal objective of every State enterprise shall be to operate as a successful business and, to this end, to be: (a) as profitable and efficient as comparable businesses that are not owned by the Crown; and (b) a good employer; and (c) an organisation that exhibits a sense of social responsibility by having regard to the interests of the community in which it operates and by endeavouring to accommodate or encourage these when able to do so.

The respective duties of the directors and of the relevant ministers of the Crown are set out in sections 5 and 6, and section 7 requires the Crown to pay for any non-commercial activity it may wish an SOE to perform. This framework is designed to reduce the scope for political interference in the business decisions of SOE managers. Part II of the Act sets out the corporate structure of the SOEs, and Part III creates reporting provisions for their accountability.

Once this framework was established, the government began corporatising its trading departments. Fourteen SOEs (including five organisations such as Air New Zealand that were already operating under a corporate structure) were established on 1 April 1987. In the following years, many of these SOEs were privatised (that is, sold to the private sector), while other trading organisations owned by the Crown were progressively converted into SOEs. At the end of June 1997 there were fifteen SOEs: Airways Corporation, Coal Corporation, Contact Energy, Crown Forestry Management, Electricity Corporation, Government Property Services, Land Corporation, Meteorological Service, New Zealand Post, Railways Corporation, Television New Zealand, Terralink, Timberlands West Coast, Trans Power, and Vehicle Testing.

While some significant transitional problems were encountered during the corporatisation and privatisation process, there is no doubt that the overall result was sustained improvements in the commercial performance of the former government organisations, spectacularly so in such cases as Telecom. Labour productivity increased, and the SOEs remaining in Crown ownership began to pay dividends and taxes reflecting their improved performance. The rise in labour productivity was initially achieved by lay-offs and staff redundancy agreements as tens of thousands of workers were declared surplus, while output levels were maintained or increased. These lay-offs, of course, contributed significantly to the sharp rise in unemployment during the economic reforms (see chapter 8).

Beyond these transitional costs, two major criticisms of the corporatisation and privatisation programme have been maintained. The first concerns the fate of the non-commercial objectives removed from the former government organisations. In most cases these objectives have been allowed to lapse, and small rural towns, for example, experienced the loss of some postal and banking services and employment opportunities as a result. As employment growth recovered in the mid 1990s, however, and as alternative service providers began to fill some of the gaps left by the rationalisation of the larger corporations, the extent of this criticism has diminished.

The second criticism concerns the degree of market power enjoyed by some of the larger corporations. During the privatisation process, some public monopolies were sold to the private sector (for example, the Natural Gas Corporation) while in some industries there remains a concern that the market dominance of the SOE or former SOE may have allowed it to earn super-normal profits (for example, in telecommunications and electricity generation). The response of the government, which has attracted some criticism, has been to encourage greater competition in and easier access to the industry concerned, rather than imposing regulatory controls on prices, and to rely on more general laws aimed at curbing anti-competitive behaviour, as discussed in the following section.

THE PROMOTION OF COMPETITION IN MARKETS

The previous section has described how the State Owned Enterprises Act 1986 created a framework within which the government's commercial operations could be corporatised in order to improve efficiency and productivity growth. Economic theory suggests that these objectives can be further promoted by allowing competition to determine market prices, since genuinely competitive markets will produce prices that reflect the opportunity cost of both production and consumption. At the change of government in 1984, many important prices in New Zealand—almost all interest rates, for example—were set by regulation rather than by market forces. In addition, many important markets were subject to legal restrictions on entry by new firms; Air New Zealand, for example, enjoyed monopoly rights for air travel on all major routes in the country. An important step towards increasing competition in New Zealand product and service markets was the reduction in import barriers phased in after 1984 (see chapter 4), but a number of significant initiatives were also undertaken to promote domestic competition.

A useful starting point for examining changes in the philosophy and practice of industry policy is the reform of the Commerce Act in 1986. The previous Commerce Act, which had passed into law in 1975, was described in its preamble as 'an Act to promote the interests of consumers and the effective and efficient development of industry and commerce through the encouragement of competition, to prevent the mischiefs that may result from monopolies, mergers and takeovers and from trade practices, to prevent strikes and lockouts against the public interest, and to provide for the regulation, where necessary, of the prices of goods and services'. In contrast, the preamble of the Commerce Act 1986 states simply that it is 'an Act to promote competition in markets within New Zealand'.

In keeping with this objective, section 27 of the new Act declares that 'no person shall enter into a contract or arrangement or arrive at an understanding, containing a provision that has the purpose, or has or is likely to have the effect, of substantially lessening competition in a market'. Similarly, section 36 declares that 'no person who has a dominant position in a market shall use that position for the purpose of: (a) restricting the entry of any person into that or any other market; or (b) preventing or deterring any person from engaging in competitive conduct in that or in any other market; or (c) eliminating any person from that or any other market'. Later in the Act, section 66 seeks to prevent mergers and takeovers that would create or strengthen a dominant position in a market, unless it 'would be likely to result in a benefit to the public which would outweigh any detriment'.

Responsibility for enforcing these provisions is given to the Commerce Commission, subject to appeal to the High Court. The Commerce Commission has significant powers of investigation and enforcement, and is permitted to grant an exemption only if it is likely to result in a benefit to the public that would outweigh the reduction in competition. 'Benefit to the public' is not defined in the Act, but the commission has tended to emphasise gains in efficiency that can occur when a larger scale of operation reduces unit costs (economies of scale) or when technological advances allow lower prices.

The same competition framework outlined in the Commerce Act 1986 was used to guide other reforms of the government's industry policy in two important aspects. First, it was decided that prices in the economy should be determined by market forces rather than by government regulation. At the beginning of 1984, thirty-nine product groups (including motor vehicles, fertilisers, butter, and soap) were subject to specific price controls, apart from the general price freeze that ended in February that year. By the end of 1992, all of these controls had been removed.

Second, it was decided that regulatory barriers to entry into certain occupations and industries were no longer appropriate since they were not consistent with the promotion of competition. The list of regulations is too long, and the occupations and industries too diverse, to analyse the impact of their removal in this short chapter, but three representative examples can be given. In 1986, Ansett New Zealand was granted approval to operate passenger flights on the main trunk routes, previously serviced by Air New Zealand alone. The public noticed an immediate impact as Air New Zealand upgraded its airport facilities and standards of service to meet the new competition. On 1 April 1987, an amendment to the Reserve Bank Act allowing new entrants into the banking industry came into effect. Eight new banks were registered in July, and others followed in later months. In 1989, quantity restrictions on taxis were replaced by quality requirements, leading to an enormous increase in the number of taxi cabs on the road (in Wellington the increase was almost 50 per cent).

Regulatory reform to promote competition in the market place is an ongoing process. The small size of the New Zealand economy, and its distance from larger markets overseas, mean that policymakers must always be concerned about possible anti-competitive behaviour by domestic enterprises. This makes the work of the Commerce Commission vitally important in monitoring and preserving fair competition in New Zealand markets.

THE IMPACT ON LABOUR PRODUCTIVITY

Graph 7.1 shows that labour productivity fell in 1985/86, but that for the next seven years its growth rate was high by recent standards: on average 2.4 per cent per annum, compared to 1.3 per cent per annum during the 1960s and early 1970s. More recently, however, the rate of productivity growth has

Graph 7.2 Output and employment growth

Description
The graph shows the percentage change of New Zealand's real gross domestic product (excluding agriculture) and the percentage change of full-time equivalent employees.

Sources
The two series come from the same sources described in graph 7.1.

slowed again, averaging just 0.25 per cent per annum between 1992/93 and 1997/98. It is also interesting to analyse the two components that make up labour productivity growth; namely, output growth and employment growth, as depicted in graph 7.2.

The graph shows that throughout the 1960s and 1970s output and employment growth followed a similar pattern over the business cycle: employment growth tended to be high when output growth was high, and their troughs also coincide. This familiar relationship in macroeconomics is named Okun's Law after the economist who first measured it for the USA in the 1960s. During the economic reforms in New Zealand, however, this relationship appeared to change. The year 1985/86 was particularly unusual in that employment growth remained moderately high although output fell (leading to the large fall in labour productivity that year). For the next seven years, real output growth fluctuated between negative 2 per cent and positive 3 per cent, but full-time equivalent employment declined year after year (by 10.9 per cent overall).

Thus, the productivity growth achieved during the transitional phase of the reforms was created by labour retrenchment rather than output growth. Under these circumstances, of course, the increase in productivity was reflected in a higher unemployment rate rather than in higher average living standards for the country.

Since 1991/92, Okun's Law appears to have been re-established. Output grew by about 6 per cent in 1993/94 and 1994/95, and employment growth was also strong at about 5 per cent. As chapter 8 will discuss, unemployment fell quickly during these two years, but as output growth slowed after 1994/95, so did employment growth. More worrying for policymakers is that labour productivity growth also slowed, raising a question mark over whether the reforms have succeeded in improving New Zealand's labour productivity growth performance on a permanent basis.

PHYSICAL CAPITAL INVESTMENT

This chapter has highlighted the importance of productivity growth for raising living standards for the community as a whole and for conserving scarce resources. While the measure used here to illustrate New Zealand trends has been labour productivity, it is important to recognise that there are other essential inputs into production that must also be efficiently managed, particularly land, natural resources, physical capital, human capital, and investment in research and development.

Historically, much productivity growth has been the result of producers implementing new and better methods of production as a result of expenditure on research and development. Many of the ideas used in New Zealand are generated overseas, but there are country-specific and product-specific questions that need to be researched domestically to produce technology appropriate to New Zealand conditions and circumstances. Before 1984, a very large percentage of domestic research and development was performed and funded by government through the universities, the Department of Scientific and Industrial Research (DSIR), and the Ministry of Agriculture and Fisheries (MAF). Concerns that this research was not organised or focused as well as it might be led to the formation of the Foundation for Research Science and Technology (FoRST) to manage the government's Public Good Science Fund for research. This initiative was intended to encourage greater participation in research by the private sector (whose participation is low by OECD standards) as well as increasing the accountability of researchers in the public sector. Raising the productivity of the researchers should increase the productivity of the industries they service.

Two other very important contributions to productivity growth are investment in physical capital (new buildings, new plant and machinery, new public infrastructure), embodying the latest technology, and investment in human capital (post-compulsory education and on-the-job training), increasing the

Graph 7.3 Investment

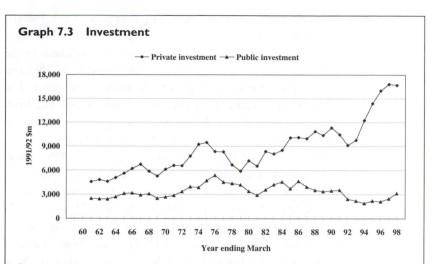

Description
The graph shows the real value of New Zealand's gross investment by the private sector and by the public sector (central and local government). This records New Zealand's gross fixed capital formation before allowance is made for the investment needed to compensate for depreciation on the existing capital stock.

Sources
Statistics New Zealand's modern series on the components of GDP begins in 1982/83. The data for real gross fixed capital formation are found in INFOS series SNBA.SWI, and the division into private and public investment comes from the nominal series in SNBA.SDB, SNBA.SDC, and SNBA.SDD. D. Grindell (ed.), *Consolidated National Accounts for New Zealand on an SNA Basis* (Wellington: Reserve Bank of New Zealand Discussion Paper No. 32, 1981), gives comparable data to 1978/79, and the intervening three years' data were derived as a residual item by subtracting the real data in graphs 4.2 and 7.2 from the real GDP data in graph 1.1.

skills of the working-age population. Human capital accumulation is notoriously difficult to measure, but physical capital accumulation is estimated as part of the system of national accounts. Graph 7.3 depicts this time series of gross investment by private firms and government organisations.

An interesting feature of the private investment series is the clear pattern of rises and falls around a generally rising trend. This pattern is an important part of explanations by economists of the 'business cycle' phenomenon apparent in most modern economies. Keynesian economists have proposed in the past that policymakers might moderate this cycle by increasing public investment when private sector investment is weak. However, graph 7.3 shows that the opposite has been typical in New Zealand, with public and private investment following very similar cycles, at least until 1983/84.

After 1983/84, public investment was constrained as part of the government's efforts to reduce the fiscal deficit. The privatisation of its trading departments further reduced the share of investment undertaken in the public sector, while a private sector investment boom between 1993/94 and 1995/96 drove the very high economic growth in those three years. The combination of these events meant that public investment, which had been 35.1 per cent of total investment in 1960/61 and as high as 41.5 per cent in 1978/79, had fallen to 11.7 per cent of total investment in 1994/95.

The private sector investment boom between 1993/94 and 1995/96 was truly outstanding, involving a 64 per cent increase in just three years. The only comparable experience occurred in the early 1970s, when private sector investment increased from about $4 billion in 1971/72 to about $6 billion in 1973/74. That boom proved to be short-lived; private sector investment had fallen back below $4 billion by 1978/79, and broke through the $6 billion mark only in 1984/85. The long-term success of New Zealand's reforms may similarly be judged by whether the recent surge in investment turns out to be temporary (the result of firms catching up on investment projects delayed during the reforms) or permanent (creating new benchmark levels of investment and hence of economic growth).

CHAPTER EIGHT

LABOUR POLICY

At the heart of every country's economic system is the work that its citizens perform. Work, of course, encompasses a very wide range of both paid and unpaid activities, and the value of work to a person's self-esteem and social standing cannot be measured simply by the income earned. Indeed, a great deal of essential work in all economies receives little or no explicit monetary compensation, particularly the work of family care, household production, and voluntary community service. This makes a government's labour policy very important, not only because it is concerned with such a core social value (human work), but also because the economic problem of integrating market and non-market work within an acceptable social framework is enormously complex.

To provide an example, the Arbitration Court in New Zealand between 1936 and 1954 was obliged by law to determine a basic wage for adult males that 'should be sufficient to maintain a man, his wife and three children in a fair and reasonable standard of comfort'. At the same time, it was accepted that women would receive lower rates of pay than men doing the same work (until the Equal Pay Act 1972 made such discrimination illegal). Nor was it unusual for women to be dismissed from their employment upon marriage— a practice now prohibited under the Human Rights Act 1977. Present-day social attitudes make such a system unthinkable, but the task of formulating appropriate labour policies is as important now as it was sixty years ago.

Another reason for paying particular attention to labour policy in this review of New Zealand's economic reforms is that this was the one area where the two major parties expressed fundamental disagreement on the proper course for reform. As this chapter will describe, the Labour Government sought to strengthen the existing framework of labour legislation through the Labour Relations Act 1987 and the Employment Equity Act 1990, while a

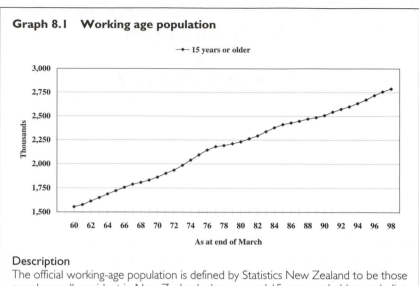

Graph 8.1   Working age population

—◆— 15 years or older

As at end of March

Description

The official working-age population is defined by Statistics New Zealand to be those people usually resident in New Zealand who are aged 15 years and older, excluding those in the armed forces or in institutions. For some purposes, researchers have also excluded those older than 65, but this has not been done in the above graph.

Sources

The Household Labour Force Survey records its estimate of the working-age population in HLFQ.SAD3AZ from December 1985. Earlier data were constructed from INFOS series DAEA.SAA and DAEA.SAB (1980/81 to 1984/85), table 3 of the *Quarterly Population Bulletin* (1976/77 to1979/80), the 1976 Census (1975/76), and tables 1 and 5 of the *Monthly Abstract of Statistics* (1959/60 to 1974/75).

cornerstone of the National Government's economic policy was the Employment Contracts Act 1991, which adopted a radical new approach.

The chapter begins with a description of historical trends in New Zealand's working-age population and the division between market and non-market work. The middle two sections then discuss the respective reforms introduced by the Labour and National governments. The final section provides an analysis of labour market outcomes in terms of employment and real wages.

HISTORICAL TRENDS

New Zealand's working age population is plotted in graph 8.1, which shows an increase of more than a million people over the last thirty-eight years. The average annual growth rate of 1.6 per cent is high by OECD standards and reflects New Zealand's relatively high birth rate. Graph 8.1 also reveals definite periods of accelerated and restrained growth around this trend. This pattern is due partly to demographic factors (for example, the impact

Graph 8.2 Participation rates

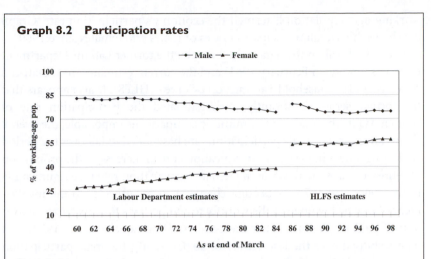

Male Female

Description

The participation rate of a country is the percentage of its working-age population who are employed or who are available for employment and actively seeking work. Those not participating in the country's labour force will typically be involved in full-time education or in full-time unpaid family care, or retired. Since women more often than men tend to be responsible for unpaid care of dependents and tend to live longer than men in retirement, the participation rate of women is below that of men in OECD countries, although the gap has declined over the last three decades.

Sources

The Household Labour Force Survey provides official estimates of participation rates for males and females from 1985/86, recorded in INFOS series HLFQ.SAE1AZ and HLFQ.SAE2AZ. Before this, the Department of Labour provided estimates of New Zealand's labour force for the end of April (1960–79) and for the end of February (1980–84) reported in the *New Zealand Official Yearbook*. These data were divided by the working-age population data in graph 8.1 to give the left-hand-side of the graph above. Note that the Department of Labour series up to 1984 and the HLFS series from 1986 cannot be compared.

of the 'baby boom' after the Second World War on the working-age population fifteen years later) and partly to migration patterns, which tend to involve inflows when the economy is performing well and outflows during recessions. Such rapid changes in migration are facilitated by the absence of restrictions on trans-Tasman migration, which creates in some respects a single Australasian labour market.

Working-age people are classified according to whether they engage in full-time or part-time market work (including active search for employment) or in full-time non-market work (including further education). The ratio of people either in or actively seeking market employment to the total working-age population is termed the economy's participation rate. Graph 8.2 shows the overall participation rates of males and females since 1960.

There is a break in the data series between the former Labour Department estimates (ending in February 1984) and the current estimates from Statistics New Zealand's Household Labour Force Survey (HLFS). It also appears that the former series significantly underestimated the participation rate of women. While this makes strict numeric comparisons impossible, the overall trends are clear. The male participation rate has tended to fall over the period (reflecting longer involvement in education and an increase in the proportion of retirement-age men), while the female participation rate rose significantly in the 1960s and 1970s (reflecting changing social attitudes to the involvement of married women in the workforce and perhaps the greater attractiveness of paid employment after the passing of the Equal Pay Act 1972), but then stabilised over the last decade or so. Currently, the male participation rate is around 75 per cent and the female rate is around 57 per cent.

It is interesting to note that the rise in the female participation rate has been balanced by the fall in the male rate. According to the Labour Department data, the aggregate participation rate was 54.9 per cent in 1960, had risen to 56.4 in 1969, but was still 56.2 per cent at the end of the series fifteen years later. The HLFS series shows that the aggregate rate declined from 66.3 per cent in 1986 to 65.6 per cent in 1998. Thus it is not reasonable to blame rising unemployment on rising female participation rates, as is sometimes done.

A more controversial hypothesis is that aggregate participation rates may be lower than they would otherwise be because of the income support provided under social welfare, particularly to domestic purposes beneficiaries. Some economists have argued that the domestic purposes benefit (DPB), introduced in 1973 to provide financial support to unemployed single parents, contributed to a dramatic rise in divorce rates and the proportion of one-parent households in New Zealand. Others have argued that the DPB was necessary to reflect social changes that have taken place in all Western countries.

Whatever the outcome of that debate, concern about the impact of benefits on participation rates involves two considerations. The first is the level of income support provided, relative to the wage that a beneficiary might expect in employment. This is known as the replacement ratio. The higher the replacement ratio, the lower the recipient's relative poverty compared to people in employment, although the participation rate of beneficiaries is also likely to be lower. The second consideration involves the way in which income support (including access to subsidised public services such as health) is reduced as a beneficiary earns extra market income. This reduction is measured by the effective marginal tax rate, defined as the total amount of benefits a beneficiary loses as a result of earning one extra dollar from employment. For domestic purposes beneficiaries the rate can be more than 90 per cent for wide ranges of market income. High effective marginal tax rates tend to discourage participation in part-time employment, creating a poverty trap for single parents.

These considerations have had an impact on government policy in recent years. The Treasury briefing papers after the 1990 general election included calculations of replacement ratios and effective marginal tax rates, and concluded: 'many beneficiaries face little incentive to reduce their dependence on the state'. The government subsequently announced significant reductions in the level of income support entitlements from 1 April 1991, by 10.7 per cent ($27.21 per week) in the case of DPB recipients with one child. Effective marginal tax rates remained high, and even increased in many cases as a result of other policy changes.

General economic conditions also have an impact on participation rates. Part of the decline in New Zealand's aggregate participation rate after 1986 may have been caused by the sharp rise in unemployment during the process of economic restructuring. For example, a person may believe that they are so unlikely to find employment during a deep recession that they no longer actively seek work, or else choose to take early retirement (the 'discouraged worker' effect). Also, a person who has been made redundant may decide that re-employment will require new skills, and so may choose to leave the workforce temporarily in order to undertake full-time education. These considerations apply to both men and women, of course, but female participation rate patterns are complicated by more complex family choices. For example, the participation rate of women of child-bearing age may increase during a period of high unemployment as some couples choose to delay starting a family until employment prospects are more certain.

INITIAL INDUSTRIAL RELATIONS REFORMS

The system of industrial relations in place at the change of government in July 1984 was based on three principles that had scarcely changed since the original Industrial Conciliation and Arbitration Act of 1894. The first principle ('exclusive rights of union representation') was that every union was required to define its membership coverage rule (normally on the basis of members' occupation) so that it did not overlap with the coverage of any other union. Thus any employed worker could belong to only one union, and in many occupations (at least up to some salary bar) union membership was also compulsory. The second principle ('blanket coverage') was that the minimum terms and conditions of employment (known as 'awards'), having been negotiated at a national level by the relevant union and employers' organisations, should be compulsory for all employers of workers in the award occupation. The third principle ('compulsory arbitration') was that the State should provide a mechanism for resolving industrial conflicts that arose either in the negotiation of awards or in subsequent enforcement of their provisions.

In practice, industrial relations centred on an annual wage round beginning in about September each year, in which individual unions negotiated changes in their awards with employers' organisations. The Metal Trades Award, the General Drivers Award, and the Electrical Contractors Award were negotiated early in the wage round, and the wage increases in these awards set the trend for subsequent negotiations based largely on a system of historical relativities between occupations. If any award negotiation broke down, it could be referred to the Arbitration Court for a binding decision. All employers of workers covered by an award were obliged to observe its minimum terms and conditions, but for some occupations in some industries, unions could negotiate above-award terms and conditions after the wage round. This 'second-tier bargaining' meant that workers with market power could increase their wages, but the award system meant that high unemployment could not reduce wages in occupations with an excess supply of available workers.

At the change of government in July 1984, New Zealand's system of industrial relations was in considerable turmoil as a result of the incomes and prices freeze, which had expired in February 1984. Because the freeze had been introduced in June 1982, before the annual wage round, most workers had not received a wage increase for three years, apart from a general wage order of $8 a week in April 1984. It was also recognised that the 20 per cent devaluation in July would further erode the real income of workers, but employer and employee groups had opposite views on whether workers should be compensated for this, given the high unemployment at the time.

The new government proceeded cautiously. It introduced a tripartite wage conference before each annual wage round to enable union, employer, and government representatives to discuss wage guidelines in the context of the state of the economy. The government also restored compulsory union membership, but removed provisions for compulsory arbitration (both parties now had to agree to refer a dispute to the Arbitration Court before the Court could intervene). Otherwise the system proceeded as before. The 1984 wage round produced settlements of around 6.0–7.5 per cent, but the 1985 round saw agreements of 15 per cent or more in the midst of considerable industrial strife. This reversed the trend of the previous three years of falling real wages (see graph 8.4), but marked the beginning of rising unemployment that did not stop until 1992/93 (see graph 2.3).

The government undertook a major review of the existing framework of private sector industrial relations throughout 1985 and 1986. This led to the Labour Relations Act 1987, which also became the legislation covering public sector workers after the passing of the State Sector Act in 1988. The preamble of the Labour Relations Act calls it 'an Act to reform the law relating to labour relations and, in particular,—(a) To facilitate the formation of effective and accountable unions and effective and accountable employers organisations; (b) To provide procedures for the orderly conduct of relations between workers and employers; (c) To provide a framework to enable agreements to be reached between workers and employers'. These aims reflected the government's decision not to alter radically the traditional principles of industrial relations, although within these principles some important changes were made.

First, registered unions were required to have a minimum of a thousand workers, which led to a series of union amalgamations; over the next three years the number of registered private and public sector unions fell by two-thirds, from 239 in March 1988 to eighty in March 1991. Second, workers who entered into enterprise agreements under second-tier bargaining were obliged to exclude their employers from coverage by the relevant award, the intention being that stronger worker groups covered by such agreements could not then be used to support wage claims in future award negotiations. Third, the Act replaced the Arbitration Court with a three-pronged approach to resolving industrial disputes: a Mediation Service to assist parties to resolve disputes on a voluntary basis; an Arbitration Commission to deal with disputes of interest (such as wage negotiations); and a Labour Court to rule on disputes of rights (such as personal grievance claims).

The overall flavour of the Labour Government's approach to industrial relations can be illustrated by two further initiatives late in its second term of office. In July 1990 the government passed the Employment Equity Act, which set up an Employment Equity Commission to promote equal employment opportunities and to redress the inequitable impact of discrimination against women in respect of their remuneration ('pay equity'). On 17 September 1990 the government announced an 'Agreement for Growth', in which the Council of Trade Unions agreed to exercise its influence to achieve wage settlements of 2 per cent plus any rise in productivity; the government undertook to reverse the deterioration in its fiscal position; and the Reserve Bank indicated its intention not to prevent any easing in monetary conditions that flowed from the wage restraint. In both cases, the government was moving towards a more corporatist approach to industrial relations, but neither initiative survived the change of government in October 1990.

THE EMPLOYMENT CONTRACTS ACT 1991

One of the first actions of the new National Government was to repeal the Employment Equity Act. Then on 19 December 1990 it announced an 'Economic and Social Initiative', which significantly reduced income support entitlements under social welfare, set up reviews of other major areas of government expenditure, and introduced legislation intended 'to bring about the most fundamental change to industrial relations in New Zealand since the inception of the Industrial Conciliation and Arbitration Act of 1894'. When the Employment Contracts Act came into force on 15 May 1991, its preamble described it as:

An Act to promote an efficient labour market and, in particular,—

(a) To provide for freedom of association:

(b) To allow employees to determine who should represent their interests in relation to employment issues:

(c) To enable each employee to choose either—

    (i) To negotiate an individual employment contract with his or her employer; or

    (ii) To be bound by a collective employment contract to which his or her employer is a party:

(d) To enable each employer to choose—

    (i) To negotiate an individual employment contract with any employee:

    (ii) To negotiate or to elect to be bound by a collective employment contract that binds two or more employees:

(e) To establish that the question of whether employment contracts are individual or collective or both is itself a matter for negotiation by the parties themselves:

(f) To repeal the Labour Relations Act 1987.

The fundamental point of departure from previous legislation is presented in the first line: whereas the Labour Relations Act 1987 had been intended 'to reform the law relating to labour relations', the Employment Contracts Act 1991 was intended 'to promote an efficient labour market'. While the new Act explicitly protects freedom of association, the previous principles of compulsory unionism and blanket coverage were replaced by a principle of voluntary negotiation between individual parties (who may choose to enter into a collective agreement but cannot bind any other parties to it). The Act also combined the Mediation Service and the Arbitration Commission into a new Employment Tribunal, and the Labour Court was renamed the Employment Court.

Under previous legislation, the primary employment relationship was between the union (to which an employee was obliged to belong) and the employers' organisation (whose agreements bound all employers). Under the Employment Contracts Act, however, the primary relationship is between the individual employee and the individual employer, with neither party able to force a collective agreement on the other.

The main objective was to increase the flexibility of individual firms and workers to negotiate the terms of their employment, in order to allow productivity gains to be identified, implemented, and rewarded—something not easily achieved with centralised bargaining. The legislation provides for certain minimum conditions to be part of every employment contract (a minimum number of statutory holidays is specified, for example, and offences such as discrimination or sexual harassment are explicitly outlawed), but otherwise the terms of any contract are a matter for negotiation by the employer and employee.

The legislation provides no special role for trade unions. Rather, workers are entitled to appoint a bargaining agent, who may be a union representative, a lawyer, or an employment contracts specialist. The employer must recognise that agent, but there is no statutory requirement for the employer to bargain in good faith with the appointed person. The Act allows employees to strike, and an employer may lock out employees, during the negotiation of an employment contract, but once agreement has been reached such industrial action is not permitted until the contract is due to expire.

The Employment Contracts Act came into force at a time when unemployment was extraordinarily high in New Zealand, which meant that employers were in a relatively strong market position. Most of the initial conflict under the Act occurred when employers sought to introduce individual contracts (with reduced real wages or changed conditions of employment) but their employees wished to maintain a collective agreement.

Employment and real wages

The previous two sections have described the core labour policy legislation introduced by the Labour and National governments respectively. Such legislation, of course, only sets out a framework within which individuals and organisations make choices and enter into employment relationships. The first section of this chapter discussed some of the factors influencing the

Graph 8.3 Employment

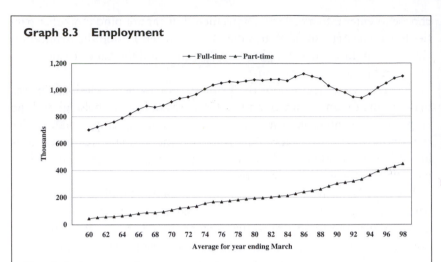

Description

The employment data used to draw this graph come from the Quarterly Employment Survey, which was carried out by the Department of Labour until 1987 and then taken over by Statistics New Zealand. Note that the data estimate the number of jobs provided by New Zealand employers (excluding the agriculture sector) rather than the number of people employed (which is estimated by the Household Labour Force Survey).

Sources

Full-time employment and part-time employment come from QESQ.SAIZ91 and QESQ.SAIZ92 respectively, after 1987/88. For earlier years, data from the Department of Labour's Quarterly Employment Survey were used, published in table 1 of *Employment Statistics, 1979–1983*, and in various issues of the *New Zealand Official Yearbook*, the *Monthly Abstract of Statistics* and *Key Statistics*.

choices people make about whether to participate in paid employment; these supply-side choices interact with the demand-side decisions of employers to determine overall outcomes in the labour market.

Two broad influences on labour demand receive special attention in economic analysis. The first is the relationship between the marginal productivity of workers compared to their real wage. If marginal productivity increases or real wages fall, it becomes more profitable for firms to employ workers, and employment should rise. The second influence is the relationship between aggregate demand for goods and services in the economy and average productivity. If aggregate demand falls (perhaps as a result of reduced exports during a world recession, or tighter domestic fiscal or monetary policies) or average productivity rises, firms need fewer workers and employment should fall. The fact that different economists put different emphases on these two influences can lead to wide disagreement in labour policy discussions.

Graph 8.4   Real wage rate

— Real wage (firms)

Index (1985 = 100)

145
130
115
100
85
70

60 62 64 66 68 70 72 74 76 78 80 82 84 86 88 90 92 94 96 98

As at March quarter

Description

The real wage rate is a concept designed to adjust the nominal wage rate paid by firms for the impact of inflation. From the perspective of firms, the real wage rate is defined as the nominal wage rate before tax divided by the price of their output goods and services. (It is also possible to define real wages from the perspective of workers; that is, the nominal wage rate after tax, divided by the consumer price index.)

Sources

In December 1992, Statistics New Zealand introduced a new labour cost index as its best measure of changes in the average cost to firms of employing one worker. This series is contained in the INFOS series LCIQ.SA5329. For earlier years, the nominal wage series was constructed using the prevailing wage index in PWIQ.S4329 for 1977/78 to 1991/92 and the nominal weekly wage index in *Prices, Wages and Labour* for 1959/60 to 1976/77. The price series for output goods and services after 1977/78 is the producers price index (outputs) in PPIQ.SO2, and for earlier years is the prices received for commodities produced in New Zealand (index in *Prices, Wages and Labour*).

Graphs 8.3 and 8.4 depict time series over the last thirty-eight years for New Zealand's employment level and average real wage rate, the two variables that appear in any standard labour market analysis. In graph 8.3, two categories of work are distinguished: full-time and part-time. Full-time jobs are much more prevalent than part-time jobs, although the graph reveals that the gap between them closed considerably during the reforms. In 1960, part-time jobs comprised 5.9 per cent of total jobs; by 1998 they had increased to nearly 29 per cent.

Two major factors caused this closure. The first was the rise in part-time jobs, a trend that is evident since 1960, but which accelerated during the policy reforms. The second was the extensive fall in full-time employment between 1986 and 1993. This contraction was very unusual; graph 8.3 shows that full-time employment had previously increased every year since 1960 (apart from the recession in 1967/68, following a major decline in New Zealand's terms of trade). The explanation can be found in the lower aggregate demand and rising average productivity during the policy reforms, which resulted in large-scale redundancies in private sector industries, SOEs, and government departments.

Graph 8.4 depicts the average real wage rate of workers, calculated from the firms' point of view; that is, the nominal wage before tax, deflated by an index of the prices of goods and services sold by the firms. Before 1968, wages were strongly influenced by a centralised wage-setting system based on national awards and overseen by the Arbitration Court, and by a hierarchical system of relativities in which stronger unions settled their terms of employment first to create a standard for weaker unions. Real wages in this era grew slowly and steadily, approximately in line with productivity growth.

Confidence in the Arbitration Court collapsed in 1968, however, when it declared a nil general wage order after the fall in New Zealand's terms of trade. Over the next twenty years, wage policy comprised a mixed system of union–employer negotiations augmented from time to time by government intervention. As graph 8.4 shows, real wages rose sharply in 1971 and again in 1975, but moved back to about their 1971 level for the rest of the decade. This was despite growing economic difficulties, falling labour productivity, and rising unemployment. After the introduction of the incomes and prices freeze in June 1982, real wages fell for three years in a row, but then jumped back up again in the 1985/86 wage round. Real wages have been relatively stable since then, although with a slight downward trend to 1994/95 despite rising productivity. That trend was in keeping with the restraint imposed by high unemployment during that period, and appears to have reversed as unemployment fell during the recovery.

CHAPTER NINE

NEW ZEALAND'S ECONOMIC PERFORMANCE, 1984–98

The previous five chapters have discussed New Zealand's economic reforms under the respective headings of international trade, monetary policy, fiscal policy, industry policy, and labour policy. Such divisions were necessary because each reform rested on different principles and dissatisfactions in each policy area. The overall impact of the reforms on economic performance, however, depended not only on each specific reform but also on their interaction. The purpose of this chapter, therefore, is to reconsider the economic reforms in chronological order and to assess their impact on the four major indicators of economic performance introduced in chapter 2. Graphs 9.1 to 9.4 depict those four indicators from March 1980 to March 1998, using quarterly rather than annual data (note, however, that the GDP Deflator inflation rate has been replaced by the CPI inflation rate because of problems with data availability). The following sections discuss New Zealand's experience during and since the reforms, with an overall evaluation at the end of the chapter.

JULY 1984 – AUGUST 1987

Chapter 3 described the sense of crisis that emerged immediately after the July 1984 general election, reinforced by the Treasury's critical analysis of previous economic management in its post-election briefing papers. In fact, the principal macroeconomic indicators had shown some improvement before the election: the sharp recession of 1983 had ended, and annual economic growth was back above 5 per cent in June 1984 (graph 9.1); inflation had been reduced to around 4 per cent from a peak of more than 16 per cent in mid 1982 (graph 9.2); unemployment was still at a very high level compared to the 1960s and 1970s, but was also showing signs of falling in June 1984 (graph 9.3); and only the balance of payments deficit appeared to be deteriorating (graph 9.4). The improvements, however, were recognised as unsustainable; economic growth, for example, was being stimulated by a record fiscal deficit accommodated by expansionary monetary policy (and accompanied by a bumper agricultural harvest), while inflation had been suppressed artificially by the incomes and prices freeze.

The new government's first act was to respond to the foreign exchange crisis by devaluing the New Zealand dollar by 20 per cent on 18 July 1984. The capital outflow during the election campaign made some action along these lines inevitable, but there were also positive reasons for a significant devaluation. In particular, it was expected to improve the competitiveness of New Zealand's tradables sector, which in turn would encourage more investment in this sector and mitigate the impact of subsequent reforms on farmers and manufacturers.

With this analysis in mind, the 1984 Budget addressed the fiscal deficit problem by announcing that most components of government assistance to producers in the form of direct and indirect subsidies would be phased out over the next few years, and that taxation would be reformed with the introduction of a new expenditure tax (GST) in 1986. A decision was also made to direct monetary policy towards reducing inflation, relying on orthodox policies of general monetary restraint rather than on particular interest rate or reserve asset ratio regulations. Indeed, the monetary sector was quickly deregulated in an attempt to introduce greater efficiency through improved private sector competition.

On 4 March 1985, New Zealand moved from a fixed to a floating exchange rate regime. This gave the Reserve Bank control over the domestic money supply, which it could use to pursue price stability. The move also meant that the process of internationalising the New Zealand economy took a major step forward.

In 1986 the government passed the State Owned Enterprises Act, which declared that the principal objective of SOEs would be to operate as a successful business, and the Commerce Act, designed to promote competition in New Zealand markets. In 1987, the Labour Relations Act sought to strengthen New Zealand's system of compulsory unionism and blanket coverage while at the same time weakening some of the links between award negotiations and second-tier bargaining. Also in 1987, the government announced a programme of state asset sales to reduce the level of gross public debt (especially its overseas debt).

Thus the government had completed a wide range of economic reforms by the time the next general election was held in August 1987. Further, these reforms did not have a particularly adverse impact on the macroeconomic indicators. Real economic growth fell sharply in the first eighteen months after the 1984 election but recovered to slightly more than 2 per cent by June 1987. While the introduction of GST temporarily pushed the inflation rate beyond 18 per cent, it was widely accepted that the core rate of inflation was closer to single figures. Unemployment was remarkably stable for more than a year at about 4 per cent, which, although high by New Zealand standards at the time, was no worse than before the previous election. Finally, the balance of payments deficit moved back from 9 per cent at the beginning of 1986 to 5 per cent in June 1987. The government won the election comfortably, increasing its majority in Parliament.

SEPTEMBER 1987 – OCTOBER 1990

Despite its landslide election victory, the Labour caucus that reconvened in Wellington contained an internal division that became increasingly disruptive as the months passed. One group of MPs believed that the economic reforms had been largely completed during the government's first term, and expected that the second term would be devoted to implementing social policies to improve equity in health, education, housing, and income distribution. Indeed, the Royal Commission on Social Policy had been appointed in October 1986 to receive public submissions and offer policy recommendations, and was due to report some time in 1988. Another group of MPs, however, believed that only the first stage of the economic reform programme had been completed, and argued that the election result had provided a mandate to accelerate the pace of reform, especially after the sharemarket crash in October 1987.

These irreconcilable differences became public when Prime Minister David Lange unilaterally announced in January 1988 that the government's pre-Christmas policy statement promising a flat income tax rate of 24 cents in the dollar would not be implemented. The chairperson of the Royal Commission on Social Policy had already expressed his concern that the government's economic policies were closing off social policy options. Consequently the Commission brought its deliberations to an early close in April 1988 with the publication of a four-volume report, which summarised the submissions it had received but failed to present an integrated set of policy recommendations.

A large part of 1988 was devoted to the public debates between the Lange and Douglas factions within Cabinet over the future of the government's economic and social policies. On 14 December 1988, Roger Douglas resigned from Cabinet, saying he could no longer work with the Prime Minister. Seven months later, however, the Labour caucus re-elected Douglas to Cabinet, whereupon Lange resigned, to be replaced by Geoffrey Palmer.

Throughout this period, the pace of reform slowed considerably. Only one piece of significant legislation was introduced in 1988: the State Sector Act, which revised the responsibilities and duties of chief executive officers (previously called permanent heads) of government departments, making them more accountable for providing agreed outputs to their ministers but also giving them greater freedom to manage their departments (for example in employment decisions). On the other hand, the government continued to make progress towards its fiscal and monetary policy objectives. GST was increased from 10 per cent to 12.5 per cent on 1 July 1989 in an effort to further reduce the fiscal deficit. The Public Finance Act 1989 moved the Crown's accounting system towards generally accepted accounting practice, laying the foundations for New Zealand's comprehensive set of public accounts discussed at the beginning of chapter 6. The Reserve Bank of New Zealand Act was also passed at the end of 1989, cementing in legislation the principle that price stability was the sole objective of monetary policy (subject to certain rare exceptions) and giving the Reserve Bank autonomy in choosing the best means of achieving and maintaining that objective.

Real economic growth in New Zealand remained below 2 per cent throughout this period, and unemployment jumped from 4 per cent to 7 per cent. Inflation had been reduced by the Reserve Bank to 4 per cent in the middle of 1989, but the increase in GST caused a temporary relapse. The balance of payments deficit had fallen almost to zero in the depths of the recession in March 1989 but was back at 4 per cent of GDP during the first nine months of 1990. Against this backdrop, the general election on 29 October 1990 produced a landslide victory to the National Party.

NOVEMBER 1990 – OCTOBER 1993

Even as the election was being held, the New Zealand economy was moving into an even deeper recession. Annual growth had slowed throughout 1990 and became negative in March 1991. Unemployment that quarter rose to 9 per cent and soon passed into double figures. Reserve Bank initiatives during 1990 to restrain inflation (following the GST increase) produced higher interest rates. All of these changes affected the government's accounts: tax revenue fell, income transfers to the unemployed rose, and interest payments on public debt increased. The Treasury therefore advised the new government that it had inherited a fiscal crisis that would produce a fiscal deficit of 6.3 per cent of GDP within three years if policies did not change.

The government's response on 19 December 1990 was to announce an economic package that reduced entitlements to income support under social welfare by about $25 per week, representing a drop in income of between 2.9 and 24.7 per cent for most beneficiaries. The benefit cuts, introduced from 1 April 1991, were expected to generate savings in social welfare spending of $1.275 billion in the 1991/92 fiscal year. The economic package also announced that the government was adopting the broad principle that the top third of all income earners could be expected to meet most of the costs of their social services. To make progress towards this goal, and to generate significant fiscal savings, it set up a series of working parties and special committees on the reform of social assistance, targeting social assistance, the funding and provision of health services, and accident compensation, and separate reviews in education, housing, and superannuation.

The result of this work was presented to Parliament in the first Budget of the new Minister of Finance, Ruth Richardson. The overall thrust of the reforms is summarised in the following paragraph from the Budget speech: 'The redesign of the welfare state is integral to our strategy for growth. We cannot make economic progress without reforming our social systems, nor can social and economic policy be divorced from one another. The only sustainable welfare state is one that is fair and affordable. Our current system is neither.'

The main philosophical change was a move away from universal provision of public services such as health and tertiary education towards targeted provision, in which higher-income individuals were expected to contribute a greater share of the cost in direct part-charges, rather than indirectly through the taxation system. The organisation of the health system underwent a major change in which the funding of health services (through Regional Health Authorities) was separated from their provision (by Crown Health Enterprises and private providers). Accident compensation costs for non-work accidents were transferred from employers to employees. Housing assistance moved from a system of subsidised rents in public housing to a system of accommodation supplements (vouchers) for low-income families, which could be used in either the private or the public sector; at the same time, public sector rents were increased to market rates. National superannuation was made subject to an incomes test, although this was later changed under a multi-party agreement to a higher age of entitlement (phased in from 60 to 65) in order to put state-funded superannuation on a more sustainable basis.

This radical reform of the fundamental principles of New Zealand's welfare state was matched by an equally radical reform of industrial relations. The third component of the December 1990 economic package was the announcement of the Employment Contracts Act. This legislation, intended to promote an efficient labour market based on individual employment contracts, came into force on 15 May 1991.

The impact of these fiscal and labour market reforms on the macroeconomic indicators was immediate. By the end of 1991, the target inflation rate of between 0 and 2 per cent had been achieved exactly two years ahead of schedule, and the balance of payments deficit was almost back to 2 per cent of GDP. Real economic growth, however, continued to shrink throughout 1991, and unemployment peaked in the September quarter at 10.9 per cent.

Recovery was initially slow but then began to gather pace. Unemployment remained above 10 per cent throughout 1992, but had moved back to 9.2 per cent by the time of the next election on 6 November 1993. Annual economic growth moved back into positive values in June 1992, and in September 1993 jumped from 2.8 to 4.4 per cent (the first time it had been above 3 per cent since 1985). In the meantime, inflation remained within the 0–2 per cent target range, while the balance of payments deficit also remained under control at around 2 per cent of GDP.

Despite these positive indicators, the National Party struggled to retain voter support in the 1993 general election and was returned with a very small majority. Further, in a referendum held at the same time, the electorate voted to change from a first-past-the-post electoral system to MMP. This vote was widely interpreted as reflecting the electorate's desire to prevent radical economic and social reforms on the scale imposed by successive governments since 1984.

November 1993 – September 1996

Prime Minister Jim Bolger responded to the close election result by deciding that Ruth Richardson would not retain her position as Minister of Finance and appointing Bill Birch in her place in a reshuffled Cabinet. This move signalled an end to New Zealand's programme of major economic reforms, with one exception. Richardson remained chairperson of the select committee responsible for introducing the Fiscal Responsibility Bill and for steering it through Parliament. The legislation set out principles of fiscal management designed to prevent a repetition of the Budget problems produced by some of the fiscal policies of her predecessors (see chapter 6).

The major theme of the 1994 Budget was 'building on the gains made so far'. For the first time since 1978 the adjusted financial balance was in surplus, making it possible to continue paying back overseas public debt without ongoing asset sales and to fund a small number of new initiatives, for example in education and health. With this approach reflected in other policy areas, the lead-up to New Zealand's first general election under MMP (due in late 1996) became a period of consolidation.

The government was rewarded by sustained growth of about 6 per cent up to March 1995 and by sharp falls in unemployment, down to 6.6 per cent. This caused some inflationary pressures and an increase in the balance of payments deficit, but the Reserve Bank took quick action to contain the former, while the latter was considered appropriate given the high level of investment (requiring imported capital goods) taking place at the time. In February 1996, the government announced a major tax reduction pro-gramme. As discussed in chapter 6, the programme involved reductions in the middle income tax rate, to be introduced in two stages from 1 July 1996 and 1 July 1997. This was promoted by the government as an example of the benefits made possible by the economic reforms, although critics pointed out that this policy would further increase the gap between high- and low-income households that had widened during the previous decade.

OCTOBER 1996 – MARCH 1998

New Zealand's first election under MMP took place on 12 October 1996. The key macroeconomic indicators for the third quarter of that year were reasonably positive. Growth had slowed from its peak of more than 6 per cent but was still very respectable at 3.1 per cent. Inflation was slightly above the Reserve Bank's target of 0–2 per cent that then prevailed, at 2.4 per cent, but showed no signs of accelerating. Unemployment had stabilised at about 6 per cent, well below its peak of 10.9 per cent five years earlier. The balance of payments deficit had widened to 3.6 per cent, but this was still considered acceptable for an economy still recovering from several years of low or neg-ative growth (between 1986 and 1993). Nevertheless, the election campaign revolved around issues of economic management, and the election itself produced a finely balanced Parliament as follows: Act New Zealand, 8 mem-bers; National, 44; New Zealand First, 17; United New Zealand, 1; Labour, 37; and Alliance, 13. National and New Zealand First entered into a formal Coalition Agreement on 10 December 1996. As chapter 6 explained, the Coalition Agreement postponed the second round of the tax cuts until July 1998 in order to allow the government to increase its spending by $5 billion over the three years of its term.

Over the next eighteen months, however, the economic indicators deterio-rated. Inflation was successfully stabilised around the middle of its widened target band of 0–3 per cent, but growth continued to slow to 2.2 per cent for the year ending March 1998. Unemployment had increased to 7.1 per cent, while the balance of payments deficit had risen above 7 per cent. The slowdown in economic activity had been in part due to a serious drought in several parts of the country (affecting agricultural production and exports) and to a fall in demand for New Zealand exports as a result of what became known as the 'Asian economic crisis'. This crisis had been building for some time, but was finally triggered on 2 July 1997 when Thailand's central bank was forced to abandon pegging its currency (the baht) to the American dollar. The baht depreciated sharply, putting similar pressures on the currencies of Indonesia, Malaysia, South Korea, and Taiwan. Economic activity in these countries contracted, causing widespread destitution and political unrest. This crisis was reinforced by problems in Japan's banking sector, which prevented that country from increasing demand in the region and by fears that a competitive devaluation by China would lead to further instability. At the time of writing (August 1998) it is still not clear how seriously the Asian economic crisis will affect New Zealand, but there is no doubt that it represents the most serious external shock to the country since the events of 1973 described in chapter 2.

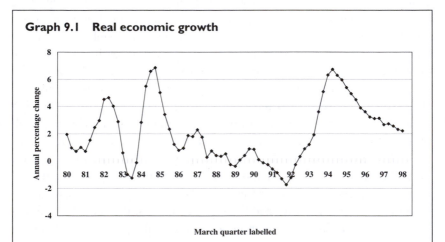

Graph 9.1   Real economic growth

March quarter labelled

Description
The graph shows the same statistic as in graph 2.1; that is, the percentage change in New Zealand's real GDP. The data have been presented on an annual basis; that is, each point on the graph records on the vertical axis the percentage increase in real GDP for the twelve months up to and including the quarter labelled, compared to its value for the previous twelve months.

Source
Real gross domestic product is taken from the INFOS series SNBQ.S2SZT.

AN OVERALL EVALUATION

New Zealand's programme of economic reforms occurred in two substantial waves during the first terms of the Labour and National governments respectively. In the first wave, the New Zealand dollar was devalued by 20 per cent and then floated on foreign exchange markets; financial markets were deregulated; product markets were opened up to greater domestic and international competition; government subsidies to private producers were phased out; income taxes were reduced and GST was introduced; government trading departments were corporatised into commercial state-owned enterprises; the privatisation programme began; monetary policy was directed towards achieving and maintaining price stability; and the task of bringing the public accounts into line with generally accepted accounting practice was begun. In the second wave of reform after 1990, key components of New Zealand's welfare state were restructured, and the labour market was deregulated under the Employment Contracts Act.

There were some interesting parallels between the two waves of reform. Both were triggered by a sense of crisis (the foreign exchange crisis of July

Graph 9.2 Consumer price inflation

Percentage change (vertical axis: 0, 3, 6, 9, 12, 15, 18, 21)

Horizontal axis: 80 81 82 83 84 85 86 87 88 89 90 91 92 93 94 95 96 97 98

March quarter labelled

Description
Data for the GDP deflator shown in graph 2.2 are not available on a quarterly basis, so this graph shows the percentage change in New Zealand's consumer price index. Each point on the graph records on the vertical axis how much the consumer price index for the quarter shown on the horizontal axis has increased on the value of the index four quarters earlier. It is thus the rate of consumer price inflation for the year ended that quarter.

Source
The consumer price index comes from the INFOS series CPIQ.SE9A.

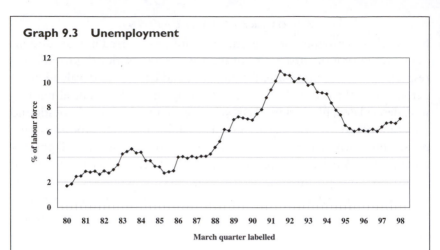

Graph 9.3 Unemployment

March quarter labelled

Description

The graph shows the same statistic as in graph 2.3; that is, the number of people not in employment who are both available for work and actively searching for a job, expressed as a percentage of the labour force. The graph shows for each quarter New Zealand's official unemployment rate obtained from the Household Labour Force Survey, adjusted statistically to remove a clear seasonal pattern in the data (since unemployment tends to be higher in the June and December quarters than in the March and September quarters). HLFS data begin in 1986, so that earlier points in the graphs are estimates only, based on registered unemployment and Quarterly Employment Survey data linked to the relevant HLFS series.

Sources

The official seasonally adjusted employed and unemployed statistics come from the INFOS series HLFQ.S1A3S and HLFQ.S1B3S respectively.

1984 and the fiscal crisis at the end of 1990). Both sets of reforms were unpopular, to the extent that both Ministers of Finance responsible came to lose the confidence of their respective Prime Ministers. The pace of reform slowed considerably in the second term of both governments, although in each case landmark legislation (the Reserve Bank of New Zealand Act 1989 and the Fiscal Responsibility Act 1994) was passed to formalise and cement reforms that had taken place earlier.

Thus the programme of economic reform was implemented over a lengthy period, from 18 July 1984 (when the New Zealand dollar was devalued) to 1 July 1994 (when the Fiscal Responsibility Act came into force). By their very nature, such radical changes were bound to cause severe disruptions to the economy's flows of income and expenditure, and this is evident in the pattern of real economic growth depicted in graph 9.1. The annual growth rate fell quickly from its peak of 7 per cent at the end of 1984, and

Graph 9.4   Balance of payments

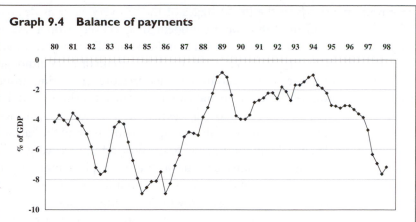

March quarter labelled

Description

The graph shows the same statistic as in graph 2.4; that is, the difference between current revenue received from the rest of the world and current payments paid to the rest of the world, expressed as a percentage of GDP. Each point on the graph records on the vertical axis this value over the previous twelve months, up to and including the particular quarter shown on the horizontal axis.

Sources

The balance of payments current account surplus comes from the INFOS series BOPQ.S4AC3 (formerly BOPQ.STOT I 69). The figure for nominal GDP is obtained from a simple linear interpolation of the year ending March data in INFOS series SNBA.SB9.

apart from a small recovery in the first half of 1987, it remained below 2 per cent from December 1985 to June 1993. Over the same period, the rate of unemployment rose from 3 per cent to nearly 10 per cent (graph 9.3).

The first tangible sign that progress was being made occurred in the December quarter of 1991, when consumer price inflation moved within its target price stability range of 0–2 per cent and remained there throughout 1992 (graph 9.2). In 1993 the balance of payments deficit moved below 2 per cent of GDP (graph 9.4), and in the 1993/94 fiscal year the government's operating deficit moved into surplus (graph 6.1), thus completing the reform programme's transition stage, which aimed at getting these three macroeconomic fundamentals into balance.

As the macroeconomic fundamentals were achieved, the level of real economic growth began to recover. Real GDP began to grow again on an annual basis in September 1992, passed above 3 per cent in September 1993, and reached six per cent in June 1994, where it remained for twelve months. The trend of rising unemployment stopped at the end of 1991, but employment improved only slowly in the initial stages of the recovery as firms delayed taking on new staff until they were confident that recovery would last. A surge in business confidence then saw unemployment fall sharply, from 9.1 per cent at the beginning of 1994 to 6.2 per cent at the end of 1995, although the fall was accompanied by a rise in inflationary pressures (requiring strong action by the Reserve Bank, which increased interest rates sharply) and a small deterioration in the balance of payments. These indicators remained stable in 1996, but 1997 saw growth fall, unemployment rise, and the balance of payments widen in a disappointing end to the post-reform recovery.

This pattern of slow or negative growth during the implementation and transition stages of a programme of extensive economic reforms, followed by a slow recovery and then stronger growth, is a common one. However, the impact of the Asian economic crisis in 1997 shows that New Zealand remains vulnerable to external shocks from the global economy. Indeed, since the post-1984 programme of reforms was founded on a desire to increase the integration of the New Zealand economy into global markets, the country's susceptibility to such shocks, both positive and negative, may have increased over the last fifteen years. The problem of economic management in a small open economy far removed from the major population centres of the world remains a very difficult one.

CHAPTER TEN

ONGOING ISSUES IN ECONOMIC MANAGEMENT

For most purposes, the programme of radical economic reform that began in New Zealand in July 1984 concluded with the passing of the Fiscal Responsibility Act in June 1994. This completed the redesign of the basic framework within which government economic management now takes place, resting on principles enshrined in landmark pieces of legislation such as the State Owned Enterprises Act, the Commerce Act, the State Sector Act, the Public Finance Act, the Reserve Bank of New Zealand Act, the Employment Contracts Act, and the Fiscal Responsibility Act. Further, the vote in the 1993 referendum to change New Zealand's electoral system from 'first past the post' to mixed-member proportional representation was widely interpreted as an indication that the electorate itself wished to slow the pace of fundamental economic reform.

Nevertheless, further change is inevitable, since economic management is always an ongoing and dynamic process. (It would be a mistake, for example, to think that there were no changes before July 1984, when in fact the phasing out of import licences began in 1981, and the first deregulation of interest rates occurred in 1976.) The electorate might support further policy changes to a wide range of economic and social issues. Some of these issues have risen out of the reform process itself, while others are enduring problems that require more work from policy advisers and economic researchers. The purpose of this chapter is to identify some of the important policy issues that are likely to be part of future economic debate.

Before we consider specific examples, however, a general observation can be made: the reform programme did not just affect certain government policies; in many important ways it also altered basic institutions of New Zealand society. If we think about 'institutions' in a very broad sense—not simply as organisations and structures, but as the whole set of social mores, rules, and conventions that guide people's behaviour and decision-making—then institutional change on the scale recently experienced in New Zealand must be viewed as cultural change. Cultural change cannot be permanently imposed on a society, but will endure only if people are generally happy with the institutions around them. Furthermore, since groups of people can change institutions and the way they function, cultural change is a continuously evolving process.

The fact that some of the institutions created during the reforms are radically different from those they replaced has created considerable tension in the community. In some cases this tension can be attributed to 'teething problems' in the new institutions, which may be resolved by some relatively minor modifications. In other cases, as the benefits of the cultural change come to be recognised, people may choose to adapt their behaviour to make the most of the new institutional environment. In still other cases, ongoing discomfort with a new institution may create pressure for a policy U-turn to restore a version of its former self. Many of the issues considered in this chapter are particular examples of this more general tension created during the decade of reform.

THE WELFARE STATE

New Zealand's welfare state before 1990 was built on principles of universal access to fully state-funded health and education; of income support at a level to allow social welfare beneficiaries a sense of participation in society; and of funding by a system of progressive taxation. During the economic reforms, policies were introduced to create a new type of welfare state, one based more on targeted provision of subsidised public services; on income support at a safety-net level to avoid extreme poverty; and on a minimalist tax system in which tax rates are kept as flat as possible. The rationale for this shift was that dramatic changes in New Zealand's economic and social position meant that the old type of welfare state was no longer affordable nor fair. It was also argued that income support at a level to allow participation in society could encourage beneficiaries to choose dependency on social welfare. On the other hand, the new system of tight eligibility criteria, with high abatement rates on additional earnings, implies high effective marginal tax rates for welfare beneficiaries. Since these create strong incentives not to seek additional work, people can become trapped on social welfare in this system too.

Another tension concerns the trade-off between the extent to which public services are made available universally and the size of the transfer payment or subsidy made to each eligible person. Given some overall budget constraint, the larger the eligible group, the smaller must be the subsidy. Alternatively, in order to raise a benefit on egalitarian grounds, eligibility has to be tightened; but questions are then raised about what criteria should be used in an ever-changing social environment and who should set the criteria.

Such issues have led many social policy analysts in New Zealand to conclude that even more fundamental questions need to be asked about the design of a modern welfare state. How can we enhance social security and social cohesion, for example, while respecting the need for economic rewards for individual effort and creativity? What should be the role of government in funding social goods such as health and education, compared to the role of individuals in paying for their own needs? To what extent can a small country like New Zealand pursue independent economic and social policies at a time when the global economy is becoming increasingly integrated? Work on these and related questions is likely to be an important focus for research in the years ahead.

POVERTY

Since modern economics began in the eighteenth century, a major motivation for economists has been the desire to better understand the causes of poverty and to find more effective mechanisms for creating and distributing wealth. Indeed, dissatisfaction with New Zealand's history of economic growth and with the economic opportunities available to certain groups in New Zealand society were major factors in the universal acceptance of the need for reform at the Economic Summit Conference in September 1984. Despite these good intentions, however, it is clear that poverty levels rose sharply during the reform programme, particularly in the early 1990s when the rate of unemployment reached double figures and the level of income support provided through social welfare was reduced by up to 24.7 per cent. The result was an enormous increase in the number of people seeking aid from private charities and foodbanks.

As employment growth recovered after 1993, some of these pressures eased, although not entirely. There is now some evidence that households experiencing unemployment are not the only ones vulnerable to poverty. Families facing increased costs in housing, health, and education can find it very difficult to make ends meet without assistance, even when at least one adult member is in permanent full-time employment. This reality, if it endures, creates new problems, because policymakers have previously been able to assume that employed people could earn sufficient market income to meet the needs of their families. If this assumption is no longer correct, then new policies or institutions will be required to avoid a situation where low-income households have no opportunity to improve their situation beyond the basic survival level.

INCOME DISTRIBUTION

The question of income distribution is an ambiguous one for economists. On the one hand, a wider income distribution can provide clear incentives for effort, creativity, and success; on the other hand, a narrower income distribution can improve social cohesion and reduce public costs in areas such as policing and justice. Recent research using official Statistics New Zealand data shows that the income distribution of households in New Zealand became more diverse during the economic reforms, largely as a result of the reduction in income tax rates in 1988 and the reduction in social welfare income support in 1991. (The international rise in real interest rates will also have had an impact, by raising the return on capital relative to labour.) Both of these policy reforms, of course, were intended to increase incentives for effort, but it is not yet clear whether there will be wider social impacts that will need to be considered by policymakers.

FISCAL POLICY

The conceptual questions raised in the previous three sections find their practical application in the area of fiscal policy. Chapter 6 recorded that the government's public accounts moved into balance in 1993/94 and recorded significant operating surpluses thereafter. While this situation opened up new possibilities for the government, it also revealed wide differences of opinion about how best to use the surpluses. The New Zealand Government Financial Statement in table 6.1 provides a framework for discussing the options.

First, the operating surpluses could be used to retire public debt in order to reduce the debt-servicing expenses on the expenditure side of the financial statement. Indeed, this has been the government's first priority, its aim being to retire public debt (especially overseas debt) until net public debt is about 20 per cent of GDP. This strategy not only reduces the government's interest commitments on its debt but also reduces its exposure to the risk of adverse currency movements affecting the domestic value of its overseas debt.

Second, the operating surpluses could be reduced by lowering taxation revenue. Within this option, there are further choices to be made; for example, whether to lower personal income tax rates, or company tax rates, or the rate of GST. In its February 1996 tax reduction programme, the government chose to reduce the middle income tax rate.

Third, the operating surpluses could be reduced by increasing transfer payments (at least in part reversing the benefit cuts of April 1991). Again there are choices about how this could be done; for example, should eligibility rules be relaxed, abatement rates on additional earnings lowered, or entitlement rates increased? There was some movement in this direction as part of the February 1996 programme, particularly for domestic purposes beneficiaries seeking part-time employment.

Fourth, the operating surpluses could be reduced by increasing government expenditure on public services such as education and health, either to provide more services or to increase the remuneration of people working in these areas. The December 1996 Coalition Agreement provided $5 billion over three years for this purpose.

It is not necessary, of course, to choose just one of these options to the exclusion of all the others; rather, future governments will continue to choose some combination of reducing debt, lowering tax rates, raising transfer payments, and increasing spending on public services. These choices will implicitly define the key characteristics of New Zealand's welfare state for the next generation, so it is not surprising that debate about the options is emerging as one of the critical economic and political issues of the late 1990s.

Superannuation

In 1977, the government introduced a universal national superannuation scheme that was funded at a significantly more generous level than earlier public schemes (see graph 6.2 and the accompanying discussion in chapter 6). Within a decade it had become obvious that New Zealand's ageing population would put enormous strains on the public accounts in the twenty-first century unless action was taken to reduce the government's superannuation commitments. Consequently, a controversial tax surcharge was imposed on other income earned beyond a certain level by national superannuitants (removed in 1997 by the coalition government); the age of entitlement was raised progressively from 60 to 65 years, and the government began to urge people to make greater private provision for their retirement.

Despite these moves, the savings rate of New Zealanders has not risen to any great degree, which raises questions about the political liability of future governments. If habits of expenditure and saving built up under the old type of welfare state do not change rapidly enough, or if the overall level of economic performance does not allow people to earn enough present income to increase their savings for the future, how will this impact on the contingent liabilities faced by future governments? The coalition government sought to address this question by proposing a compulsory retirement savings scheme, but this proposal was decisively rejected in a national referendum on the issue. This outcome has left a vacuum in retirement income policy that cannot be avoided indefinitely.

EDUCATION AND HEALTH

Graph 6.2 records that government expenditure on education and health is a very significant component of the New Zealand economy, accounting for about 11.5 per cent of GDP each year (compared to about 7.5 per cent in the 1960s). There are considerable pressures to increase expenditure on these public services, as the demands of a modern market economy require a more highly educated workforce, and as an ageing population requires more expensive health care made available by technological advances in medical science. These pressures are raising important issues for policy-makers in all developed economies, not just in New Zealand.

One of the important causes of persistent unemployment and under-achievement in New Zealand's labour market, particularly among certain social groups, is a large skill deficit. Skill acquisition in New Zealand between 1938 and 1984 was strongly biased by employer demand for workers equipped to operate in a highly protected economy. The industries most supported by the import substitution policy of that era tended to be low-value-added, low-technology assembly industries, involving relatively unskilled work. Margins for skill and knowledge in the labour market also tended to be low. Accordingly, people in this environment acquired minimal training by the standards of other rapidly growing industrialised economies in the OECD region. With the greater internationalisation of the New Zealand economy produced by the reforms, margins for skill in employment now reflect more closely those of world markets. This changed environment creates new challenges for education policy.

On the demand side, major changes are required in the way individuals and their families organise their lives, especially concerning the educational investments they make. Such adjustment is not a simple process, particularly for households at the lower end of the income spectrum who have little discretionary income. Māori, Pacific Island people, and single parents are heavily overrepresented in this group, and thus face extra difficulties in making the skill transition to the new market environment. On the supply side, educational institutions are also having to adjust to the new environment: course curricula are changing, and new teaching and learning methods are being introduced. But again there are critics who argue that change is not happening fast enough, and blame the inertia built up in larger educational institutions (and the Crown agencies that administer them) under the old regime.

A central question being asked at all levels of education (pre-school, primary, secondary, and tertiary) is how should educational institutions be managed to ensure that the education they provide is of the highest possible quality and relevant to their students? Is Crown ownership, monitored by a central agency, the best option, or would local or regional ownership be more efficient and produce more equitable outcomes? Is there a role for private sector organisations in evaluating school and university performance? Should government funding go to the education providers in annual budgets, or should parents or students receive funding entitlements (education vouchers) to allocate as they choose? What should be the respective contributions of private and public funding for post-compulsory education and training?

Continued health reforms seem likely for similar reasons. Policymakers are struggling to find the right policy mix that will improve both the quality and the equity of health services provided while containing overall health expenditure. Core health services have not been defined—and it is difficult to do so when advances in medical and pharmaceutical science are constantly creating new health services that were not possible even five years ago. Expenditure restraint thus involves a strategic process of ongoing negotiation between policymakers, health managers, health providers, and the associated health lobbies.

In 1991 the government sought to improve the system of health management by separating the functions of health funding and health provision. Since then, a series of major institutional restructurings has occurred with further changes likely. The new health management system continues to come under fire from health lobbies and from powerful medical practitioner associations, who claim that some of the improved efficiency has been achieved by sacrificing standards of health care. Some economists also point out that policymakers have stopped short of making health service provision fully contestable. Meanwhile, public displeasure with long waiting lists continues. The health reforms are thus at a very interesting stage in their development, providing a particularly clear example of the complex dynamics of any major cultural change.

Treaty of Waitangi claims

One of the factors affecting the government's future fiscal position is its obligation to address historical grievances between the Crown and Māori tribes. This obligation arises from the second clause of the Treaty of Waitangi (signed on 6 February 1840, at the beginning of organised colonisation in New Zealand), in which the Crown confirmed and guaranteed to Māori 'the full exclusive and undisturbed possession [the phrase used in the Māori text is 'te tino rangatiratanga'] of their Lands and Estates Forests Fisheries and other properties which they may collectively or individually possess so long as it is their wish and desire to retain the same in their possession'. During the process of colonisation, the Crown on numerous occasions failed to guarantee 'te tino rangatiratanga', but instead participated in acts of war, unjust confiscation, unhonoured conditions of sale, legal trickery, and statutory dispossession against certain Māori tribes.

In December 1985, the government passed legislation to allow the Waitangi Tribunal to hear claims brought by Māori individuals and groups against the Crown on the basis of these historical grievances. The tribunal has the power to rule on the historical facts and to make recommendations to government on how a grievance might be resolved, but has no power to impose resolutions. Rather, the government set up the Office of Treaty Settlements through which it negotiates settlements with claimants on an individual basis, often using the findings of the Waitangi Tribunal as a reference point.

At the end of 1994, the government sought to put a cap on its Treaty of Waitangi liabilities by announcing that all historical grievances would be settled from a 'fiscal envelope' of $1 billion, to be available over a period of about ten years. The announcement caused a considerable outcry, both from those who argued that the amount was far too generous given the size of the Māori population, and those who claimed it was hopelessly inadequate given the extent of the injustices suffered by Māori. Among economists, there is a wider consensus that an appropriate settlement of the historical claims would provide Māori tribes with an economic base, which could then contribute to revitalising Māori economic development devastated by the alienation of Māori land and resources during colonisation.

MONETARY POLICY

Graphs 5.2 and 9.2 reveal that by the end of 1991 the Reserve Bank had successfully reduced CPI inflation to its target range of 0–2 per cent but that this was not sufficient to prevent increasing inflationary pressures in late 1994 and early 1995. The mechanisms currently available to the Reserve Bank to offset such pressures involve raising short-term interest rates, which attracts a greater capital inflow into the country, which in turn causes an increase in the trade-weighted exchange rate. This can reduce CPI inflation directly by reducing the price of imported goods and services, and also has an indirect impact by increasing the competitive pressure on New Zealand-made goods and services in the tradables sector (that is, exports and import substitutes).

This mechanism raises equity issues, however, since its effects are felt most strongly in the tradables sector, whereas the inflationary pressure often comes from the non-tradable sector, perhaps the result of rising property prices or housing costs. In order to maintain its credibility (and thus reduce the deflationary action needed to offset any emerging inflation), and to avoid the disinflation costs should inflation again become entrenched in the domestic economy, it is essential that the Reserve Bank continues to direct monetary policy towards maintaining price stability. Nevertheless, the search for more efficient mechanisms by which to restrain inflation without unduly affecting growth through unnecessary increases in the real exchange rate is an ongoing topic for economic research.

PRODUCTIVITY GROWTH

The observation was made in chapter 7 that the productivity growth rates achieved during the economic reforms did not continue after 1992/93 (see graph 7.1). One of the major issues confronting a wide cross-section of institutions, be they commercial firms, hospitals, universities, or government itself, is the need to continually raise quality standards and labour productivity. Many of the institutional changes during the reforms were designed to facilitate this process and to make managers more accountable for their efforts.

As with any such initiative, however, there tends to be a lot of learning by doing. In particular, it is often argued that systems introduced into New Zealand from overseas are frequently inefficient because we cannot implement procedures in exactly the same way as in other countries. Our own systems have to develop over time. There is always a danger that basically sound ideas, such as the Resource Management Act 1991 and new quality management systems in health and education, may require too many resources or may involve too many unintended compliance costs on society to be sustainable in such a small economy. This is another fertile area for ongoing economic research.

COMPETITION POLICY

The previous range of strict government regulations to restrain uncompetitive behaviour in domestic markets has been replaced by the Commerce Act, with its general prohibition on activities that reduce competition. Under this relatively light-handed approach, businesses must develop a whole new culture in their approach to competition. What is permissible is not strictly defined in the statutes, but evolves and is clarified over time by decisions made by the courts (that is, by case law). The relative importance of each decision is reinforced by the level of penalty imposed for illegal behaviour. Hence policymakers must continually review whether the evolving case law is adequate to ensure that market competition develops rapidly enough and with equity. There are questions too concerning the most appropriate format for hearing cases under the Commerce Act; for example, should they always be full court hearings, or would tribunals or other forms of public enquiry reduce the cost of administering competition policy?

A more general problem arises from the observation that most industrial technology is designed in larger countries for larger economies. This means that New Zealand is prone to the development of industries in which one or two large firms dominate because they are able to reduce their costs by increasing output, and in these cases the assumed losses from reduced competition have to be weighed against the efficiency gains from exploiting economies of scale. This is particularly important in export industries, where a prohibition on mergers to preserve domestic competition may lead to a situation where the industry cannot compete in international markets. This has led many economists to comment that the Commerce Act puts too great an emphasis on competition at the expense of a more proper emphasis on economic efficiency.

In certain 'network industries' (the telephone network of Telecom, for example), the government has determined that 'natural monopolies' must share essential facilities with competitors. This leaves open the question of what price the monopolist should be permitted to charge. In an important case involving strong monopoly elements, the Privy Council has supported the Baumol-Willig rule, under which the monopolist charges a competitor the monopoly price to share a facility, on the basis of economic theory that the presence of competitive new entrants will cause the monopoly price to fall towards the competitive price over time. It remains to be tested in practice whether the dynamics of price adjustment using this rule will ensure sufficient market competition in New Zealand to promote growth.

LABOUR POLICY

Chapter 8 explained how the principles underlying the Employment Contracts Act were radically different from those of earlier industrial relations legislation. Once again, the cultural change required by such a transformation in approach has led to considerable social tension. When the Act was introduced, unemployment was very high (nearly 10 per cent), so there was relatively little scope for that tension to produce conflict in the labour market. If unemployment continues to fall after the 1998 recession, however, it will be interesting to observe whether certain key occupational groups will be able to use their industrial strength to recoup some of the losses of real income (adjusted for productivity growth) and working conditions accepted during the recession of 1990–92 and, if so, whether this will lead to pressure for adjustments to the Act.

On the other hand, it is reasonable to suggest that the Employment Contracts Act was an important factor in allowing a rapid fall in unemployment once the economic recovery gathered pace, and that the freedom it allows for individual employers and employees to negotiate wage growth, based on improvements in productivity, is very desirable. If this is so, the fundamental principles of the Employment Contracts Act are likely to endure, although changes in some of the details of their application cannot be ruled out.

INTERNATIONAL TRADE

Even during the policy reform process, changes were being made in international trade law and in New Zealand's relations with other countries that will significantly affect our future. In multilateral affairs, the conclusion of the Uruguay round of negotiations under the General Agreement on Tariffs and Trade (GATT) produced the most comprehensive GATT agreement ever, signed in Marrakesh in 1994. Agricultural trade was included for the first time, with some limited provisions to reduce agricultural protectionism around the world. Agricultural protectionism has been very damaging to New Zealand's interests in the past, so there is potential in this agreement for a significant boost to agricultural exports. The Uruguay round also addressed other issues with important ramifications for New Zealand, such as intellectual property rights and international trade in services. A new World Trade Organisation (WTO) was created to address an extended agenda including crucial environmental issues, the rise of protectionism (through the use of non-tariff barriers such as anti-dumping taxes), the multi-fibre agreement (which heavily penalises Asian countries), air transport arrangements, and international tax laws.

New Zealand is also pursuing bilateral economic relations, especially with its four largest trading partners: Australia, Japan, the United States, and the European Union. It also has regional opportunities to pursue through the Association of South-East Asian Nations (ASEAN) and with the Asian Pacific Economic Cooperation Agreement (APEC), based on the Bogor Declaration of free trade in the region by 2010. Nor should New Zealand forget its special relations with Pacific Island nations, currently reflected in the South Pacific Regional Trade and Economic Cooperation Agreement (SPARTECA). It has been suggested, for example, that the Closer Economic Relations Trade Agreement between Australia and New Zealand (ANZCERTA, or simply CER) might be extended to include Pacific Island nations.

Such global dynamics demand continuing responses and initiatives from New Zealand individuals, firms, and organisations, including the Ministry of Foreign Affairs and Trade. New Zealand has very little leverage in international affairs and relies heavily on cooperation with other smaller countries with similar trading interests. A notable success along these lines has been the setting up of the 'Cairns Group' of countries to promote greater liberalisation of international trade in agricultural markets.

Within New Zealand, the 1984 reforms accelerated the removal of import licensing and began a process of import tariff reductions. By 1992 New Zealand had no licensing, and its tariffs were at about the same level as Australia's and only slightly higher than those of other OECD countries. More recently, tariffs have continued to be reduced, for example on imported cars. The 1998 Budget speech also announced that the prohibition on parallel importing of goods protected by copyright would be removed. Previously, the Copyright Act 1994 had banned parallel imports of copyright materials for resale, including tapes, software, books, and compact discs, even where such imports were legal copies purchased from licensed distributors overseas. Parallel import restrictions have the potential to add considerably to the cost of these items and to misallocate domestic resources in much the same way as do tariffs and import licensing, so this has been an important step in New Zealand's programme of trade liberalisation.

CONCLUSION

In a very famous quote written sixty years ago, the founder of modern macroeconomics, Maynard Keynes, observed that 'the ideas of economists and political philosophers, both when they are right and when they are wrong, are more powerful than is commonly understood'. The reforms in New Zealand between 1984 and 1994 bear ample witness to this comment. Not only were economists (particularly those employed in the Treasury and the Reserve Bank) very influential in setting out the principles used to guide most of the reforms, but people trained in economics are also employed in a wide range of New Zealand organisations to interpret the changing environment and so help decisionmakers to recognise both the new opportunities and the new problems opened up by the reform programme. Thus it is an exciting time to be an economist.

In this book, however, we have attempted to show that it is not simply economic ideas that are important. The motivation for New Zealand's reforms arose from a universal dissatisfaction in 1984 with the country's economic performance, as summarised in the data presented in this text. On this basis, the success of the reforms will be judged not by the power of the ideas that guided them but by the extent to which they lead to a measurable improvement in the lives of all New Zealanders. Similarly, we believe that the most important contribution economists can make to the ongoing process of policy development in New Zealand is to continue presenting careful empirical analyses of New Zealand data, informed by coherent economic theories judged to be appropriate to our own experience. The scope for economic research along these lines is almost unlimited.

FURTHER READING

The best New Zealand economic history from the first arrival of European settlers is Gary Hawke's *The Making of New Zealand* (Cambridge: Cambridge University Press, 1985). Economic histories concentrating on the 1960s and 1970s are provided by *A Decade of Change*, edited by Peter Lane and Paul Hamer (Wellington: Reed, 1973), *Trade, Growth and Anxiety* by Harvey Franklin (Wellington: Methuen, 1978), and *The Rake's Progress*, by John Gould (Auckland: Hodder & Stoughton, 1982). More recently, Brian Easton has written a book on New Zealand's economic history since the Second World War, *In Stormy Seas: The Post-War New Zealand Economy* (Dunedin: Otago University Press, 1997).

In the early 1980s, a number of influential publications advocated economic reform. The most influential was the briefing papers of the New Zealand Treasury at the general election of 1984, published under the title *Economic Management* (Wellington: Government Printer, 1984). Later that year, a team of economists produced for the Economic Summit Conference in September *A Briefing on the New Zealand Economy* (Wellington: Government Printer, 1984), which provided the inspiration for the title and format of this book. The New Zealand Planning Council published a series of reports in the early 1980s advocating market liberalisation; for example *The Stabilisation Role of Fiscal Policy* (1980), *Foreign Exchange Constraints, Export Growth and Overseas Debt* (1983), *Strategy for Growth* (1984), and *The Foreign Exchange Market* (1985). Relatively sympathetic accounts of the previous style of economic management were presented by John Gould, *The Muldoon Years* (Auckland: Hodder & Stoughton, 1985), and by Sir Robert Muldoon, *The New Zealand Economy: A Personal View* (Auckland: Endeavour Press, 1985).

The best accounts of the processes by which the newly elected Labour Government came to decide on the nature of its economic reforms can be found in the essays contained in Brian Easton's edited volume, *The Making of Rogernomics* (Auckland: Auckland University Press, 1989). Colin James has addressed the wider social, political, and economic factors in two very interesting books: *The Quiet Revolution: Turbulence and Transition in Contemporary New Zealand* (Wellington: Allen & Unwin, and Port Nicholson Press, 1986) and *New Territory: The Transformation of New Zealand 1984–1992* (Wellington: Bridget Williams, 1992).

During the reforms, several collections of essays were published in which contributors reviewed one or more aspects. In most cases, the title of the edited volume clearly describes the relevant subject area:

Alan Bollard and Robert Buckle (eds), *Economic Liberalisation in New Zealand* (Wellington: Allen & Unwin, 1987).

Jonathan Boston (ed.), *The State Under Contract* (Wellington: Bridget Williams, 1995).

Jonathan Boston and Paul Dalziel (eds), *The Decent Society? Essays in Response to National's Economic and Social Policies* (Auckland: Oxford University Press, 1992).

Jonathan Boston and Martin Holland (eds), *The Fourth Labour Government*, 1st and 2nd edns (Auckland: Oxford University Press, 1987 and 1990).

Jonathan Boston, John Martin, June Pallot, and Pat Walsh (eds), *Reshaping the State: New Zealand's Bureaucratic Revolution* (Auckland: Oxford University Press, 1991).

John Deeks and Nick Perry (eds), *Controlling Interests: Business, the State and Society in New Zealand* (Auckland: Auckland University Press, 1992).

Raymond Harbridge (ed.), *Employment Contracts: New Zealand Experiences* (Wellington: Victoria University Press, 1993).

Richard Le Heron, Stephen Britton, and Eric Pawson (eds), *Changing Places in New Zealand: A Geography of Restructuring* (Christchurch: New Zealand Geographical Society, 1992).

Reserve Bank of New Zealand (ed.), *Financial Policy Reform* (Wellington: Reserve Bank, 1986).

Brian Roper and Chris Rudd (eds), *State and Economy in New Zealand* (Auckland: Oxford University Press, 1993).

Ron Sandrey and Russell Reynolds (eds), *Farming Without Subsidies: New Zealand's Recent Experience* (Wellington: GP Books, 1990).

John Savage and Alan Bollard (eds), *Turning It Around: Closure and Revitalization in New Zealand Industry* (Auckland: Oxford University Press, 1990).

Andrew Sharp (ed.), *Leap into the Dark: The Changing Role of the State Since 1984* (Auckland: Auckland University Press, 1994).

Simon Walker (ed.), *Rogernomics: Reshaping New Zealand's Economy* (Auckland: NZCIS, 1989).

Tim Wallace and Ralph Lattimore (eds), *Rural New Zealand—What Next?* (Lincoln University: Agribusiness and Economics Research Unit, 1987).

Other books published during the reforms were written by one or more authors with a particular focus; for example:

Penelope Brook, *Freedom at Work: The Case for Reforming Labour Law in New Zealand* (Auckland: Oxford University Press, 1990).

Peter Brosnan, David Smith, and Pat Walsh, *The Dynamics of New Zealand Industrial Relations* (Auckland: John Wiley, 1990).

Peter Brosnan and Frank Wilkinson, *Low Pay and the Minimum Wage* (Wellington: New Zealand Institute of Industrial Relations Research, 1989).

John Deeks, Jane Parker, and Rose Ryan, *Labour and Employment Relations in New Zealand*, 2nd edn (Auckland: Longman Paul, 1994).

Ian Duncan and Alan Bollard, *Corporatization and Privatization: Lessons from New Zealand* (Auckland: Oxford University Press, 1992).

Richard Harris and Bridget Daldy, *Labour Market Adjustment in New Zealand* (Aldershot, UK: Avebury, 1994).

Prue Hyman, *Women and Economics: A New Zealand Feminist Perspective* (Wellington: Bridget Williams, 1994).

Jane Kelsey, *Rolling Back the State: Privatisation of Power in Aotearoa/New Zealand* (Wellington: Bridget Williams, 1993).

Tony Rayner and Ralph Lattimore, *Liberalising Foreign Trade*, Vol. 6, *New Zealand* (Oxford: Basil Blackwell, 1991).

Ian Shirley, Brian Easton, Celia Briar, and Srikanta Chatterjee, *Unemployment in New Zealand* (Palmerston North: Dunmore Press, 1990).

David Thompson, *Selfish Generations? The Ageing of New Zealand's Welfare State* (Wellington: Bridget Williams, 1991).

Charles Waldegrave and Rosalyn Coventry, *Poor New Zealand: An Open Letter on Poverty* (Wellington: Platform Publishing, 1987).

After the benefit cuts took place in April 1991, several community groups published material recording the impact of increased poverty in New Zealand: for example, *Neither Freedom nor Choice* (People's Select Committee, 1992); *Windows on Poverty* (New Zealand Council of Christian Social Services, 1992); *Poverty and Hardship* (Manukau City Council, 1992); and *Making Ends Meet* (Citizens Advice Bureaux, 1992). In July 1993, ten church leaders published a Social Justice Statement, followed by a book edited by Ruth Smithies and Helen Wilson exploring some of the issues raised, *Making Choices: Social Justice for Our Times* (Wellington: Church Leaders' Social Justice Initiative, 1993).

In 1994 Stephen Edwards and Sir Frank Holmes produced a publication, *CER: Economic Trends and Linkages* (Wellington: National Bank of New Zealand and Institute of Policy Studies), that presented a number of data series for Australia and New Zealand, drawing some very interesting comparisons between the two countries' approaches to economic restructuring (reflecting debates that have been a feature in two Australian general elections). More recently, two authors have written overviews of the entire reform process for an international audience: one written by a relatively sympathetic observer, Patrick Massey, *New Zealand: Market Liberalisation in a Developed Economy* (London: Macmillan, 1995), and one written by a strong critic, Jane Kelsey, *The New Zealand Experiment: A World Model for Structural Adjustment?* (Auckland: Auckland University Press and Bridget Williams, 1995; 2nd edn, 1997). Three recent collections of essays that evaluate the overall impact of the reforms are the following:

Jonathan Boston, Paul Dalziel, and Susan St John (eds), *Redesigning the Welfare State in New Zealand: Policies, Problems and Prospects* (Auckland: Oxford University Press, 1999).

Chris Rudd and Brian Roper (eds), *The Political Economy of New Zealand* (Auckland: Oxford University Press, 1997).

Brian Silverstone, Alan Bollard, and Ralph Lattimore (eds), *A Study of Economic Reform: The Case of New Zealand* (Amsterdam: North-Holland, 1996).

Three of the key ministers responsible for introducing the reforms have written on their experiences: Roger Douglas, *Towards Prosperity* (with Louise Callen; Auckland: David Bateman, 1987) and *Unfinished Business* (Auckland: Random House, 1993); Ruth Richardson, *Making a Difference* (Christchurch: Shoal Bay Press, 1995); and Richard Prebble, *I've Been Thinking* (Auckland: Seaview Publishing, 1996). Graham Scott, former Secretary to the New Zealand Treasury, has written a substantial review of the reform of the public sector, 'Government reform in New Zealand' (Occasional Paper 140, International Monetary Fund, Washington, DC, 1996). An evaluation of the entire reform programme is undertaken by Lew Evans, Arthur Grimes, Bryce Wilkinson, and David Teece in 'Economic reform in New Zealand 1984–95: The pursuit of efficiency', *Journal of Economic Literature*, Vol. 34(4), December 1996. A critique of some of that article by Paul Dalziel ('New Zealand's economic reforms, 1984–95') and a reply by the original authors is presented in the March 1998 volume of

Victoria Economic Commentaries, published by the School of Economics and Finance at Victoria University of Wellington.

Official economic commentary is provided on a regular basis by two significant sources: the government's advisers in the New Zealand Treasury and the Reserve Bank of New Zealand. The Treasury publishes Economic and Fiscal Outlooks twice during the year as part of the reporting requirements of the Fiscal Responsibility Act 1993. The Reserve Bank publishes important articles in its *Reserve Bank Bulletin* (published quarterly) and issues a *Monetary Policy Statement* four times a year as part of the reporting requirements of the Reserve Bank of New Zealand Act 1989. Both organisations also provide briefing papers to the Minister of Finance after each general election and have well-established home pages on the world-wide web (www.treasury.govt.nz and www.rbnz.govt.nz).

The Economic Summit Conference Secretariat published two volumes of *Proceedings and Conference Papers* in 1984, which provide interesting insights into the attitudes of different economic and social groups to economic reform at the beginning of the reform process. Mention should also be made of the Royal Commission on Social Policy's *April Report*, published in four volumes by the Government Printer in 1988, although this report had little subsequent influence on policymakers. The papers accompanying the 1991 Budget are very important for analysing the principles that were used to reform social policy; particularly *Social Assistance: Welfare that Works* (Wellington: Government Printer, 1991), released by the Minister of Social Welfare, Jenny Shipley.

The New Zealand Planning Council and its various monitoring groups produced a number of reports on economic and social trends until it was disbanded in 1991. Every year or two, the Paris-based OECD publishes an *Economic Survey of New Zealand*. The New Zealand Institute of Economic Research publishes *Quarterly Predictions* every three months, as well as a series of research monographs. Many of these monographs provide data and analysis of economic issues that are not available anywhere else. Similarly, the Institute of Policy Studies at Victoria University Wellington has published some important studies of critical issues that were raised during the reforms. Recent examples include the following books.

George Barker, *Income Distribution in New Zealand* (1996).

John Creedy, *Statics and Dynamics of Income Distribution in New Zealand* (1997).

Sholeh Maani, *Investing in Minds: The Economics of Higher Education in New Zealand* (1997).

Tim Maloney, *Benefit Reform and Labour Market Behaviour in New Zealand* (1997).

David Robinson (ed.), *Social Capital and Policy Development* (1997).

Certain lobby groups have produced regular reports advocating policies in one direction or another, with the most notable example being the New Zealand Business Roundtable (made up of chief executive officers of New Zealand's largest companies). This organisation regularly publishes the speeches and political submissions of its staff and members, and commissions research in support of market liberalisation; for example:

Erwin Diewert and Denis Lawrence, *The Marginal Costs of Taxation in New Zealand* (1994).

David Green, *From Welfare Society to Civil Society: Towards Welfare That Works in New Zealand* (1996).

David Henderson, *Economic Reform: New Zealand in an International Perspective* (1996).

Kenneth Minnogue, *Waitangi: Morality and Reality* (1996).

For a wealth of information on New Zealand social and economic statistics, the *New Zealand Official Yearbook* (Wellington: Statistics New Zealand) should be consulted. The 1990 issue was a special edition to mark the sesquicentennial anniversary of the signing of the Treaty of Waitangi and so contains a great deal of interesting historical information. Statistics New Zealand produces a large number of publications presenting and explaining economic data. Its *Key Statistics* is available monthly (except January), and it maintains an extensive databank called INFOS (also available as PC-INFOS for personal computers), which provided most of the data series in this book. Much of the latest data are available on Statistics New Zealand's world-wide web home page (www.stats.govt.nz).

Two academic journals that contain a number of relevant articles are *New Zealand Economic Papers* and *New Zealand Journal of Industrial Relations*. The *British Review of New Zealand Studies* has also featured several articles analysing aspects of New Zealand's economic reforms. More recently, two new journals have been launched by New Zealand government agencies, the *Social Policy Journal of New Zealand* and the *Labour Market Bulletin*, to provide a forum for further research in important policy issues.

A number of macroeconomic textbooks have been written by New Zealand authors. Jerry Mushin's *Income, Interest Rates and Prices* (Palmerston North: Dunmore Press, 1994) presents core macroeconomic theory in a concise, easy-to-follow style. Paul Wooding, *Macroeconomics: A New Zealand Introduction*, 2nd edn (Sydney: Prentice Hall, 1997), and Robert Scollay and Susan St John, *Macroeconomics and the Contemporary New Zealand Economy*

(Auckland: Addison Wesley Longman, 1996), present macroeconomic theory within a specifically New Zealand context. *The New Zealand Economy: Issues and Policies*, 3rd edn (Palmerston North: Dunmore Press, 1997), edited by Stuart Birks and Srikanta Chatterjee, contains a collection of introductory essays on important sectors in the New Zealand economy. At a more advanced level, Graeme Wells has written a book with a strong Australasian background, *Macroeconomics* (Melbourne: Nelson, 1995).

A book written by a New Zealand author that is receiving international attention for its challenge to the entire economic framework used to measure national income (reflected in graphs 1.1, 2.1, 7.1, and 9.1, for example) is *Counting for Nothing: What Men Value and What Women are Worth* (Wellington: Allen & Unwin and Port Nicholson Press, 1988) by Marilyn Waring (who was one of the two National Government backbenchers whose support for nuclear-free legislation in June 1984 led the Prime Minister to call the early election one month later, heralding the beginning of New Zealand's economic reforms).

DATA APPENDIX

NOTE: Definitions and sources for each data series can be found in the text accompanying the graph referred to at the bottom of the column. Some columns of data comprise two linked series, which are explained in the text. Every care has been taken to ensure that the data are the official statistics at the time of preparation, but readers are advised that many of the data are subject to future revisions by Statistics New Zealand. The statistics for 1998 in particular should be regarded as provisional.

Readers should also be aware that there are many ways of measuring such economic concepts as inflation or unemployment. The definitions adopted here are all standard, but have been chosen to illustrate particular points and will not necessarily be useful for all purposes. Readers looking for New Zealand data for research or econometric purposes are therefore advised to refer to the original data sources as described in the text.

Data year	Real GDP series (1995 $m)	Mean population (000)	Real per capita GDP (1995 $)	Terms of trade (index)	US real rate of interest (%)	Real economic growth (%)	Australian economic growth (%)
1960	34617	2345.6	14758	131.7	4.1	3.9	–
1961	36744	2388.0	15387	120.5	3.5	6.1	–
1962	37973	2441.4	15554	116.2	4.7	3.3	–0.4
1963	39136	2498.4	15665	123.6	3.3	3.1	6.4
1964	41522	2550.1	16282	138.0	1.6	6.1	6.6
1965	44059	2601.2	16938	140.8	0.4	6.1	6.3
1966	46744	2647.2	17658	136.8	2.2	6.1	5.6
1967	48516	2694.7	18004	133.5	1.3	3.8	3.1
1968	48098	2735.2	17585	116.4	0.5	–0.9	6.6
1969	49123	2760.1	17797	112.7	1.5	2.1	5.9
1970	51603	2788.8	18503	113.7	3.3	5.0	5.9
1971	53514	2831.2	18901	106.6	2.2	3.7	6.3
1972	54875	2876.0	19080	115.1	–0.3	2.5	5.2
1973	57307	2931.3	19550	134.9	–5.1	4.4	3.5
1974	61419	2993.6	20517	155.3	–4.9	7.2	5.0
1975	63895	3057.8	20896	108.2	3.6	4.0	2.2
1976	64970	3111.3	20882	91.3	0.7	1.7	2.9
1977	65064	3136.1	20747	98.9	–1.2	0.1	3.7
1978	63268	3143.5	20127	100.2	–1.2	–2.8	0.9
1979	63505	3143.1	20204	106.1	–0.8	0.4	3.2
1980	65126	3138.0	20754	109.8	1.4	2.6	4.7
1981	65825	3146.7	20919	98.2	7.7	1.1	2.3
1982	69060	3161.2	21846	98.8	13.5	4.9	3.6
1983	69502	3189.5	21791	95.8	10.3	0.6	–0.6
1984	71406	3230.6	22103	96.1	10.9	2.7	1.0
1985	74929	3259.3	22989	94.6	8.2	4.9	7.0
1986	75507	3273.4	23067	92.2	5.9	0.8	4.7
1987	77094	3281.6	23493	95.6	5.5	2.1	2.2
1988	77413	3310.2	23386	105.9	6.1	0.4	4.4
1989	77111	3318.3	23238	112.3	6.0	–0.4	3.8
1990	77764	3336.5	23307	117.4	7.1	0.8	4.2
1991	77306	3373.1	22919	110.9	7.4	–0.6	1.2
1992	76360	3416.0	22354	108.4	5.4	–1.2	–1.3
1993	77271	3452.6	22380	110.9	3.8	1.2	2.7
1994	82154	3492.0	23526	112.6	5.5	6.3	3.9
1995	86577	3540.7	24452	112.3	6.5	5.4	5.4
1996	89701	3597.3	24936	109.9	6.5	3.6	4.1
1997	92106	3657.3	25184	109.0	6.5	2.7	3.7
1998	94116	3696.7	25460	108.3	5.3	2.2	2.7
Graph	1.1	1.1	1.1	1.2	1.3	2.1	2.1

Data year	Nominal GDP ($m)	GDP deflator index (index)	GDP deflator inflation (%)	Australia deflator inflation (%)	QES employed (000)	Registered unemployed (000)	Estimated labour force (000)
1960	2466	30.1	2.9	–	868.2	0.6	868.8
1961	2669	30.7	2.0	–	888.1	0.3	888.4
1962	2765	30.8	0.2	1.6	903.6	0.8	904.4
1963	2998	32.4	5.2	0.8	921.8	0.9	922.7
1964	3270	33.3	2.8	3.1	949.9	0.6	950.5
1965	3582	34.4	3.2	3.0	983.1	0.6	983.7
1966	3862	34.9	1.6	2.9	1017.7	0.4	1018.1
1967	4033	35.1	0.6	2.8	1043.4	1.0	1044.4
1968	4212	37.0	5.3	3.4	1026.9	8.5	1035.4
1969	4469	38.4	3.9	3.3	1050.2	2.8	1053.0
1970	4941	40.5	5.3	5.1	1080.9	1.4	1082.3
1971	5614	44.3	9.6	3.7	1102.0	1.4	1103.4
1972	6623	51.0	15.0	7.1	1109.5	4.7	1114.2
1973	7605	56.1	10.0	7.7	1138.8	2.5	1141.3
1974	8855	60.9	8.6	12.2	1181.4	0.7	1182.1
1975	9752	64.5	5.9	17.7	1195.3	3.1	1198.4
1976	11305	73.5	14.0	15.8	1207.7	4.9	1212.6
1977	13670	88.8	20.7	13.3	1216.5	4.1	1220.6
1978	14970	100.0	12.6	9.1	1234.4	22.0	1256.4
1979	16958	112.9	12.9	7.3	1248.3	25.0	1273.3
1980	19795	128.5	13.8	10.1	1264.1	25.7	1289.8
1981	22992	147.6	14.9	11.0	1263.1	39.8	1302.9
1982	27891	170.7	15.6	9.5	1283.0	46.7	1329.7
1983	31409	191.0	11.9	11.3	1269.1	56.3	1325.4
1984	34839	206.2	8.0	8.3	1283.0	75.5	1358.5
1985	39346	221.9	7.6	6.9	1257.3	60.3	1317.6
1986	45282	253.5	14.2	5.5	1353.2	51.2	1404.4
1987	54725	300.0	18.4	6.8	1341.3	70.7	1412.0
1988	61641	336.5	12.2	8.0	1346.4	91.0	1437.4
1989	66454	364.2	8.2	8.6	1312.7	130.7	1443.4
1990	70773	384.6	5.6	7.6	1304.9	149.4	1454.3
1991	72248	395.0	2.7	4.6	1291.1	166.9	1458.0
1992	72277	400.0	1.3	2.3	1268.4	202.4	1470.8
1993	74578	407.9	2.0	1.4	1274.8	217.4	1492.2
1994	80786	415.6	1.9	1.3	1335.5	206.1	1541.6
1995	86577	422.6	1.7	1.1	1411.3	176.9	1588.2
1996	91739	432.2	2.3	2.5	1460.8	153.3	1614.1
1997	95816	439.7	1.7	2.2	1515.5	154.6	1670.1
1998	98565	442.6	0.7	1.9	1550.7	172.0	1722.7
Graph	2.2	2.2	2.2	2.2	2.3	2.3	2.3

Data year	Registered unempl. rate (%)	HLFS employed (000)	HLFS unem- ployed (000)	HLFS labour force (000)	Official unemployed rate (%)	Australian unempl. rate (%)	BoP current surplus ($m)
1960	0.1					–	81
1961	0.0					1.3	−109
1962	0.1					2.9	−112
1963	0.1					2.3	−46
1964	0.1					1.9	−30
1965	0.1					1.6	−37
1966	0.0					1.5	−186
1967	0.1					1.7	−173
1968	0.8					1.9	−110
1969	0.3					1.8	25
1970	0.1					1.8	12
1971	0.1					1.6	−227
1972	0.4					1.9	2
1973	0.2					2.6	153
1974	0.1					2.3	−84
1975	0.3					2.7	−1367
1976	0.4					4.9	−1017
1977	0.3					4.7	−786
1978	1.8					5.6	−694
1979	2.0					6.4	−471
1980	2.0					6.1	−825
1981	3.1					6.0	−823
1982	3.5					5.7	−1628
1983	4.2					7.1	−1914
1984	5.6					9.9	−1923
1985	4.6					8.9	−3358
1986	3.6					8.1	−4049
1987	5.0	1547.8	64.0	1611.9	4.0	8.0	−2824
1988	6.3	1550.5	69.5	1620.0	4.3	8.0	−2370
1989	9.1	1492.8	98.0	1590.7	6.2	7.1	−559
1990	10.3	1470.4	112.4	1582.8	7.1	6.1	−2815
1991	11.4	1479.3	135.7	1615.0	8.4	7.0	−1958
1992	13.8	1457.9	172.5	1630.5	10.6	9.5	−1881
1993	14.6	1470.4	165.6	1636.0	10.1	10.7	−1252
1994	13.4	1510.1	155.4	1665.5	9.3	10.9	−814
1995	11.1	1578.5	128.1	1706.6	7.5	9.7	−2644
1996	9.5	1648.1	108.5	1756.7	6.2	8.6	−2832
1997	9.3	1692.0	111.9	1803.9	6.2	8.5	−4520
1998	10.0	1693.8	124.3	1818.1	6.8	8.6	−7074
Graph	2.3	2.3	2.3	2.3	2.3	2.3	2.4

Data year	BoP current surplus (% GDP)	Australia current surplus (% GDP)	Nominal exchange rate (index)	Real exchange rate (index)	Real exports 1991/92$ ($m)	Real imports 1991/92$ ($m)	Public overseas debt (% GDP)
1960	3.3	–	150.5	110.7	–	–	11.1
1961	–4.1	–6.5	150.5	108.7	5239	6486	9.5
1962	–4.1	0.8	150.5	110.0	5704	6521	10.1
1963	–1.5	–3.4	150.5	112.5	5723	6380	10.5
1964	–0.9	0.0	150.4	113.4	6381	7313	9.8
1965	–1.0	–3.6	150.3	113.1	6154	7681	9.2
1966	–4.8	–5.4	150.4	111.0	6375	8941	8.6
1967	–4.3	–2.9	150.4	107.1	6909	9478	9.7
1968	–2.6	–4.1	140.9	103.2	6850	7721	11.9
1969	0.6	–4.2	131.1	96.1	7778	7712	11.5
1970	0.2	–2.6	131.2	96.1	8808	8551	10.6
1971	–4.0	–2.4	131.3	99.6	8867	10130	10.3
1972	0.0	–1.9	130.6	105.1	9522	10087	9.9
1973	2.0	1.6	135.2	112.1	9773	11040	7.4
1974	–0.9	–0.3	150.5	125.0	9528	13483	5.3
1975	–14.0	–3.5	147.7	113.0	9317	15353	8.8
1976	–9.0	–1.8	129.0	95.9	10596	12025	12.9
1977	–5.7	–2.0	123.1	99.8	11887	12209	13.4
1978	–4.6	–2.6	122.6	101.4	11908	12036	16.3
1979	–2.8	–4.2	122.6	104.2	12268	11936	17.2
1980	–4.2	–1.6	114.3	98.9	12674	13412	18.0
1981	–3.6	–3.8	107.9	98.7	13300	12512	18.4
1982	–5.8	–5.6	100.0	100.0	13686	13907	19.9
1983	–6.1	–4.0	95.8	103.2	14337	14157	24.7
1984	–5.5	–3.8	89.6	98.3	15210	14045	23.6
1985	–8.5	–5.6	75.7	89.2	16636	15665	31.5
1986	–8.9	–6.5	75.2	95.3	16912	15904	32.5
1987	–5.2	–5.1	70.0	97.1	17689	16227	39.7
1988	–3.8	–3.7	74.5	113.7	18982	17633	28.0
1989	–0.8	–4.8	72.8	114.5	19115	17495	25.0
1990	–4.0	–6.8	71.0	111.0	18647	19924	29.1
1991	–2.7	–4.9	69.5	106.0	19837	19852	28.4
1992	–2.6	–3.3	65.8	100.4	21683	19103	28.7
1993	–1.7	–3.8	62.4	92.5	22233	20516	26.6
1994	–1.0	–3.4	64.7	97.9	23999	22151	20.9
1995	–3.1	–5.9	67.7	102.9	26024	25309	15.1
1996	–3.1	–4.7	72.4	108.9	26705	27150	10.6
1997	–4.7	–4.1	77.5	117.9	27709	29025	6.6
1998	–7.2	–3.8	75.1	115.3	28387	30423	7.1
Graph	2.4	2.4	4.1	4.1	4.2	4.2	4.3

Data year	Total overseas debt (% GDP)	Nominal money supply ($m)	Growth in M3 (%)	Consumer price index (index)	Consumer price inflation (%)	Nominal interest rate (%)	Urban house prices (index)
1960		2071	9.1	73	1.4	–	–
1961		2200	6.3	74	1.4	5.3	67
1962		2211	0.5	76	2.7	5.5	68
1963		2343	6.0	77	1.3	5.6	69
1964		2561	9.3	79	2.6	5.7	72
1965		2748	7.3	83	5.1	5.9	76
1966		2857	3.9	85	2.4	6.3	80
1967		3003	5.1	89	4.7	6.5	83
1968		3115	3.7	93	4.5	6.8	84
1969		3341	7.2	98	5.4	6.8	87
1970		3645	9.1	103	5.1	6.7	92
1971		3921	7.5	113	9.7	7.3	101
1972		4326	10.3	123	8.8	8.1	114
1973		5332	23.3	130	5.7	8.1	140
1974		6157	15.5	144	10.8	8.5	201
1975		6326	2.7	163	13.2	8.9	221
1976		7404	17.0	191	17.2	10.2	234
1977		8559	15.6	217	13.6	11.2	251
1978		9698	13.3	248	14.3	11.7	253
1979	36.7	11881	22.5	274	10.5	12.1	263
1980	36.6	13744	15.7	324	18.2	13.8	281
1981	35.5	15699	14.2	374	15.4	15.4	333
1982	38.7	18329	16.8	433	15.8	16.5	450
1983	48.8	20498	11.8	488	12.7	17.3	487
1984	49.2	22901	11.7	505	3.5	12.9	549
1985	70.4	26274	14.7	572	13.3	17.5	622
1986	67.5	32386	23.3	647	13.1	19.9	682
1987	77.4	38543	19.0	765	18.2	20.5	791
1988	66.2	43835	13.7	834	9.0	16.6	919
1989	59.9	45307	3.4	867	4.0	15.2	966
1990	75.0	45961	1.4	928	7.0	14.9	1055
1991	85.0	51847	12.8	970	4.5	12.6	1067
1992	86.6	57731	11.3	978	0.8	9.9	1048
1993	91.6	61307	6.2	987	0.9	8.9	1081
1994	89.8	65332	6.6	1000	1.3	7.9	1171
1995	80.8	69726	6.7	1040	4.0	11.0	1310
1996	82.2	77950	11.8	1063	2.2	11.5	1478
1997	83.1	86624	11.1	1082	1.8	9.1	1588
1998	100.4	92677	7.0	1096	1.3	11.2	1625
Graph	4.3	5.1	5.1	5.2	5.2	5.3	5.3

Data year	Real interest rate (%)	Budget surplus table 2 ($m)	Budget surplus table 2 (% GDP)	Financial surplus table 2 ($m)	Financial surplus table 2 (% GDP)	Operating surplus GAAP ($m)	Operating surplus GAAP (% GDP)
1960	–	–95	–3.9				
1961	3.8	–80	–3.0				
1962	4.0	–67	–2.4				
1963	1.3	–122	–4.1				
1964	0.1	–107	–3.3				
1965	0.6	–89	–2.5				
1966	2.5	–114	–3.0				
1967	5.3	–134	–3.3				
1968	3.2	–110	–2.6				
1969	1.0	–109	–2.4				
1970	–3.1	–78	–1.6				
1971	–5.6	–81	–1.4				
1972	–14.7	–72	–1.1	108	1.6		
1973	–35.4	–206	–2.7	7	0.1		
1974	–1.4	–242	–2.7	1	0.0		
1975	3.0	–390	–4.0	43	0.4		
1976	3.0	–1002	–8.9	–178	–1.6		
1977	10.4	–506	–3.7	115	0.8		
1978	7.8	–694	–4.6	16	0.1		
1979	5.3	–1446	–8.5	–697	–4.1		
1980	–4.7	–1027	–5.2	–411	–2.1		
1981	–19.8	–1525	–6.6	–909	–4.0		
1982	8.3	–2026	–7.3	–1237	–4.4		
1983	4.5	–2158	–6.9	–1442	–4.6		
1984	–0.4	–3101	–8.9	–2276	–6.5		
1985	7.9	–2784	–7.1	–2000	–5.1		
1986	3.9	–1871	–4.1	–1186	–2.6		
1987	4.3	–1953	–3.6	–1830	–3.3		
1988	11.5	467	0.8	–1322	–2.1		
1989	6.0	1733	2.6	–954	–1.4		
1990	13.8	2843	4.0	–943	–1.3		
1991	14.4	1758	2.4	–2341	–3.2		
1992	6.8	–1234	–1.7	–1904	–2.6		
1993	0.6	–7	0.0	–1789	–2.4	–819	–1.1
1994	–4.0	739	0.9	424	0.5	755	0.9
1995	–1.8					2695	3.1
1996	4.1					3314	3.6
1997	6.8					1908	2.0
1998	–					2778	2.8
Graph	5.3	6.1	6.1	6.1	6.1	6.1	6.1

Data year	Social security expend. ($m)	Govt education expend. ($m)	Govt health expend. ($m)	Total govt expend. ($m)	Gross public debt (% GDP)	Net public debt (% GDP)	Real private consum. ($m)
1960	204	79	92	811	68.5		–
1961	219	88	102	874	65.0		–
1962	226	94	108	901	65.4		23357
1963	227	104	117	935	64.5		24252
1964	238	114	126	1001	61.8		25940
1965	245	130	139	1082	59.7		26876
1966	256	142	153	1169	58.4		28432
1967	267	158	167	1272	59.8		29620
1968	286	175	174	1288	62.1		28404
1969	298	188	184	1346	62.1		29097
1970	322	209	206	1466	58.2		30703
1971	356	268	245	1598	53.6		32143
1972	392	335	292	1862	48.1	6.8	32290
1973	527	377	343	2219	46.1	6.7	34524
1974	647	440	401	2633	42.2	5.1	37355
1975	790	527	492	3411	43.1	5.1	38988
1976	997	627	606	4386	49.2	8.7	38961
1977	1159	699	689	4504	46.0	7.8	38071
1978	1569	808	809	5669	50.0	8.9	37594
1979	1854	929	980	6848	52.0	15.2	38548
1980	2175	1009	1136	7587	52.3	16.3	38974
1981	2590	1292	1356	9133	50.5	17.8	39381
1982	3042	1493	1601	11197	51.6	21.3	39946
1983	3744	1639	1766	12673	59.6	28.5	39616
1984	4049	1674	1805	14250	62.8	31.8	40843
1985	4458	1729	1912	15318	71.8	40.8	42433
1986	5449	2010	2309	17672	70.7	42.7	43014
1987	6479	2595	2957	20945	77.6	46.4	44809
1988	7792	3118	3388	23117	63.5	41.5	45902
1989	9123	3569	3639	23741	59.6	45.0	46705
1990	10320	4068	3782	25508	62.7	50.5	46861
1991	11005	4401	3986	27252	60.8	47.2	46740
1992	10620	4467	3855	29174	65.2	52.7	45806
1993	12071	4539	4168	31429	63.7	49.8	45946
1994	11479	4627	4602	29639	57.5	43.8	47422
1995	11724	4803	4886	30400	50.9	37.6	50301
1996	12240	4949	5228	31743	45.2	31.2	52369
1997	12679	5335	5626	32953	37.5	26.4	54495
1998	13237	5643	6013	34318	37.4	24.7	56250
Graph	6.2	6.2	6.2	6.2	6.3	6.3	6.4

Data year	Real public consum. ($m)	Labour produc- tivity ($)	Real output growth (%)	FTE employmt growth (%)	Real private invest. ($m)	Real public invest. ($m)	Working age population (000)
1960	–	42744	4.0	1.9	–	–	1553
1961	5128	43846	6.3	3.6	4566	2473	1575
1962	5203	44036	3.4	3.0	4813	2432	1613
1963	5470	44244	2.9	2.4	4603	2410	1650
1964	5644	45266	6.3	3.9	5071	2691	1686
1965	5855	46099	6.4	4.4	5625	3108	1719
1966	6366	46791	6.0	4.5	6216	3167	1755
1967	7014	47029	3.8	3.3	6743	2927	1788
1968	6671	47058	−1.1	−1.2	5869	3071	1807
1969	6821	47182	2.1	1.8	5267	2510	1830
1970	6863	47988	5.4	3.7	6131	2672	1861
1971	7140	48182	3.8	3.4	6596	2872	1902
1972	7356	48726	2.5	1.4	6574	3348	1935
1973	8233	50092	5.2	2.4	7769	3949	1986
1974	8102	51478	7.7	4.8	9238	3861	2041
1975	8787	51646	3.6	3.3	9464	4713	2095
1976	9167	51733	1.5	1.3	8330	5359	2146
1977	9134	51107	0.1	1.4	8294	4521	2181
1978	9570	49846	−2.7	−0.2	6677	4348	2193
1979	10035	49624	0.7	1.1	5891	4174	2211
1980	9993	50108	2.1	1.1	7179	3388	2231
1981	10715	50508	0.5	−0.3	6524	2908	2264
1982	11173	52690	5.2	0.9	8354	3582	2293
1983	10812	52755	0.4	0.3	8054	4204	2338
1984	11107	54870	3.3	−0.7	8515	4540	2378
1985	11309	55788	5.0	3.2	10068	3720	2412
1986	11505	54411	−0.2	2.3	10106	4638	2429
1987	11583	56340	2.2	−1.3	9968	3931	2446
1988	11746	56631	−0.4	−0.9	10876	3514	2471
1989	11882	58767	0.0	−3.6	10378	3366	2484
1990	12185	60498	1.4	−1.5	11319	3458	2508
1991	12272	60449	−1.6	−1.5	10458	3546	2544
1992	12266	61154	−1.3	−2.4	9128	2410	2574
1993	12633	62593	2.3	−0.1	9764	2197	2600
1994	12497	63442	5.5	4.1	12240	1896	2634
1995	12380	63742	5.8	5.3	14379	2189	2673
1996	12732	63898	3.7	3.4	15995	2111	2718
1997	13006	63068	2.3	3.7	16819	2453	2756
1998	13833	63182	2.1	1.9	16692	3128	2787
Graph	6.4	7.1	7.2	7.2	7.3	7.3	8.1

Data year	Male participation (%)	Female participation (%)	Full-time jobs (000)	Part-time jobs (000)	Nominal labour cost (index)	Producer ouput prices (index)	Real wage of firms (index)
1960	83.0	26.9	700	44	11.3	14.4	78.5
1961	83.1	27.7	722	51	11.5	14.0	82.0
1962	82.3	27.8	742	56	11.7	13.9	84.0
1963	82.2	27.8	760	58	12.1	14.0	86.6
1964	82.3	28.5	788	64	12.3	15.0	82.0
1965	83.0	29.6	821	70	13.3	15.2	87.4
1966	83.1	31.0	854	81	13.6	15.6	86.7
1967	83.2	31.7	880	89	14.3	15.4	92.9
1968	82.2	30.6	870	87	14.6	15.9	92.1
1969	82.3	31.2	883	93	15.6	16.7	93.6
1970	82.5	32.2	911	107	16.7	17.3	96.6
1971	81.7	32.7	936	121	21.2	18.6	113.9
1972	80.1	33.1	947	126	23.6	20.2	116.8
1973	80.0	33.8	967	134	25.6	24.7	103.8
1974	80.1	35.3	1007	155	28.8	26.3	109.2
1975	79.2	35.4	1037	167	33.7	25.4	132.5
1976	77.7	35.2	1051	167	37.2	31.2	119.2
1977	76.1	35.9	1063	174	43.7	38.6	113.1
1978	76.8	36.0	1057	181	47.5	42.7	111.4
1979	76.2	37.2	1067	188	55.5	48.3	114.8
1980	76.3	37.9	1077	194	65.0	57.8	112.5
1981	76.2	38.2	1073	195	77.3	66.8	115.7
1982	76.1	38.5	1079	202	90.8	77.5	117.2
1983	75.0	38.6	1080	209	91.9	83.9	109.5
1984	74.2	38.8	1070	213	91.9	87.2	105.5
1985	HLFS	HLFS	1101	227	100.0	100.0	100.0
1986	79.3	53.9	1122	241	116.8	109.3	106.9
1987	78.9	54.5	1102	250	127.1	120.3	105.7
1988	76.9	54.3	1085	262	137.4	127.3	107.9
1989	75.4	53.0	1030	283	144.1	136.8	105.3
1990	74.2	53.6	1002	303	150.1	145.4	103.2
1991	74.2	54.6	981	310	155.6	145.5	107.0
1992	74.0	54.1	948	321	157.4	147.4	106.8
1993	73.3	53.6	940	335	159.0	152.2	104.5
1994	73.9	55.1	970	365	160.5	155.2	103.5
1995	74.4	55.4	1017	394	162.6	157.7	103.1
1996	75.1	56.8	1050	411	165.8	159.1	104.2
1997	74.7	57.2	1087	428	169.4	160.0	105.9
1998	74.7	57.0	1102	448	172.6	160.5	107.5
Graph	8.2	8.2	8.3	8.3	8.4	8.4	8.4

Quarter	Real GDP for quarter (index)	Annual real GDP growth (%)	Consumer price index (index)	Quarter	Real GDP for quarter (index)	Annual real GDP growth (%)	Consumer price index (index)
Mar 80	15631	1.9	324	Mar 89	18330	−0.4	867
Jun 80	15475	1.0	338	Jun 89	18568	0.1	877
Sep 80	15486	0.7	350	Sep 89	18381	0.4	908
Dec 80	15770	1.0	363	Dec 89	18332	0.9	919
Mar 81	15633	0.7	374	Mar 90	18324	0.8	928
Jun 81	16004	1.5	389	Jun 90	18336	0.1	944
Sep 81	16182	2.5	404	Sep 90	18355	−0.1	954
Dec 81	16390	3.0	420	Dec 90	18399	−0.3	964
Mar 82	16604	4.5	433	Mar 91	18076	−0.6	970
Jun 82	16641	4.6	455	Jun 91	17912	−0.9	971
Sep 82	16512	4.0	471	Sep 91	17999	−1.3	974
Dec 82	16300	2.9	484	Dec 91	18145	−1.7	973
Mar 83	16110	0.6	488	Mar 92	18213	−1.2	978
Jun 83	16244	−1.0	493	Jun 92	18182	−0.3	980
Sep 83	16670	−1.2	497	Sep 92	18069	0.3	984
Dec 83	16951	−0.1	501	Dec 92	18304	0.9	986
Mar 84	17550	2.8	505	Mar 93	18581	1.2	987
Jun 84	17571	5.5	516	Jun 93	18975	1.9	993
Sep 84	17557	6.6	531	Sep 93	19356	3.6	998
Dec 84	17822	6.9	548	Dec 93	19553	5.1	1000
Mar 85	17851	5.0	572	Mar 94	19866	6.3	1000
Jun 85	17853	3.4	601	Jun 94	20130	6.7	1004
Sep 85	17726	2.3	618	Sep 94	20395	6.3	1016
Dec 85	17925	1.2	632	Dec 94	20626	6.0	1028
Mar 86	17850	0.8	647	Mar 95	20787	5.4	1040
Jun 86	18248	0.9	664	Jun 95	20993	4.9	1050
Sep 86	18557	1.9	686	Sep 95	21125	4.5	1052
Dec 86	17976	1.8	747	Dec 95	21258	3.9	1058
Mar 87	18202	2.3	765	Mar 96	21520	3.6	1063
Jun 87	18264	1.7	790	Jun 96	21566	3.2	1071
Sep 87	18334	0.3	802	Sep 96	21782	3.1	1077
Dec 87	18363	0.7	819	Dec 96	21930	3.1	1085
Mar 88	18307	0.4	834	Mar 97	21880	2.7	1082
Jun 88	18247	0.3	840	Jun 97	22207	2.7	1083
Sep 88	18240	0.5	848	Sep 97	22312	2.6	1088
Dec 88	18169	−0.3	858	Dec 97	22402	2.3	1094
Mar 89	18330	−0.4	867	Mar 98	22191	2.2	1096
Graph	9.1	9.1	9.2	Graph	9.1	9.1	9.2

Quarter	Consumer price inflation (%)	Total employed (000)	Total unempl. (000)	Quarter	Consumer price inflation (%)	Total employed (000)	Total unempl. (000)
Mar 80		1475	26	Mar 89	4.0	1472	111
Jun 80		1472	28	Jun 89	4.4	1461	114
Sep 80		1438	36	Sep 89	7.1	1468	113
Dec 80		1459	37	Dec 89	7.1	1473	112
Mar 81	15.4	1467	43	Mar 90	7.0	1480	111
Jun 81	15.1	1471	42	Jun 90	7.6	1487	120
Sep 81	15.4	1459	43	Sep 90	5.1	1484	126
Dec 81	15.7	1483	40	Dec 90	4.9	1475	142
Mar 82	15.8	1478	44	Mar 91	4.5	1472	153
Jun 82	17.0	1491	42	Jun 91	2.9	1463	165
Sep 82	16.6	1477	46	Sep 91	2.1	1456	179
Dec 82	15.2	1485	52	Dec 91	0.9	1453	173
Mar 83	12.7	1466	65	Mar 92	0.8	1460	173
Jun 83	8.4	1471	68	Jun 92	0.9	1470	165
Sep 83	5.5	1457	71	Sep 92	1.0	1464	169
Dec 83	3.5	1477	67	Dec 92	1.3	1472	169
Mar 84	3.5	1483	68	Mar 93	0.9	1476	160
Jun 84	4.7	1517	59	Jun 93	1.3	1487	163
Sep 84	6.8	1502	58	Sep 93	1.4	1505	153
Dec 84	9.4	1529	52	Dec 93	1.4	1515	153
Mar 85	13.3	1544	51	Mar 94	1.3	1533	153
Jun 85	16.5	1569	44	Jun 94	1.1	1547	141
Sep 85	16.4	1551	45	Sep 94	1.8	1567	132
Dec 85	15.3	1562	47	Dec 94	2.8	1591	127
Mar 86	13.1	1543	64	Mar 95	4.0	1610	113
Jun 86	10.5	1546	65	Jun 95	4.6	1624	109
Sep 86	11.0	1548	63	Sep 95	3.5	1640	106
Dec 86	18.2	1540	65	Dec 95	2.9	1656	110
Mar 87	18.2	1558	64	Mar 96	2.2	1673	109
Jun 87	19.0	1559	66	Jun 96	2.0	1686	109
Sep 87	16.9	1556	66	Sep 96	2.4	1700	113
Dec 87	9.6	1555	69	Dec 96	2.6	1691	109
Mar 88	9.0	1533	77	Mar 97	1.8	1691	116
Jun 88	6.3	1516	84	Jun 97	1.1	1693	122
Sep 88	5.7	1495	99	Sep 97	1.0	1692	123
Dec 88	4.8	1489	97	Dec 97	0.8	1697	122
Mar 89	4.0	1472	111	Mar 98	1.3	1694	129
Graph	**9.2**	**9.3**	**9.3**	**Graph**	**9.2**	**9.3**	**9.3**

Quarter	Unem- ployment rate (%)	BoP current surplus ($m)	Annual BoP surplus (% GDP)	Quarter	Unem- ployment rate (%)	BoP current surplus ($m)	Annual BoP surplus (% GDP)
Mar 80	1.7	−137	−4.2	Mar 89	7.0	285	−0.8
Jun 80	1.9	−135	−3.7	Jun 89	7.2	−408	−1.2
Sep 80	2.5	−416	−4.1	Sep 89	7.1	−1333	−2.4
Dec 80	2.5	−279	−4.4	Dec 89	7.1	−1162	−3.8
Mar 81	2.9	7	−3.6	Mar 90	7.0	89	−4.0
Jun 81	2.8	−267	−3.9	Jun 90	7.5	−429	−4.0
Sep 81	2.9	−588	−4.4	Sep 90	7.8	−1144	−3.7
Dec 81	2.6	−480	−5.0	Dec 90	8.8	−566	−2.9
Mar 82	2.9	−293	−5.8	Mar 91	9.4	181	−2.7
Jun 82	2.7	−715	−7.2	Jun 91	10.1	−314	−2.5
Sep 82	3.0	−787	−7.7	Sep 91	10.9	−912	−2.2
Dec 82	3.4	−482	−7.5	Dec 91	10.6	−553	−2.2
Mar 83	4.2	70	−6.1	Mar 92	10.6	−103	−2.6
Jun 83	4.4	−258	−4.5	Jun 92	10.1	248	−1.8
Sep 83	4.6	−708	−4.2	Sep 92	10.3	−1153	−2.1
Dec 83	4.3	−570	−4.3	Dec 92	10.3	−1004	−2.7
Mar 84	4.4	−387	−5.5	Mar 93	9.8	657	−1.7
Jun 84	3.7	−768	−6.7	Jun 93	9.9	225	−1.7
Sep 84	3.7	−1221	−7.9	Sep 93	9.2	−1014	−1.5
Dec 84	3.3	−1043	−8.9	Dec 93	9.2	−787	−1.2
Mar 85	3.2	−326	−8.5	Mar 94	9.1	762	−1.0
Jun 85	2.7	−735	−8.1	Jun 94	8.4	−353	−1.7
Sep 85	2.8	−1329	−8.1	Sep 94	7.8	−1209	−1.9
Dec 85	2.9	−897	−7.5	Dec 94	7.4	−1101	−2.2
Mar 86	4.0	−1088	−8.9	Mar 95	6.6	19	−3.1
Jun 86	4.0	−626	−8.3	Jun 95	6.3	−437	−3.1
Sep 86	3.9	−933	−7.1	Sep 95	6.1	−1369	−3.2
Dec 86	4.0	−702	−6.4	Dec 95	6.2	−992	−3.1
Mar 87	3.9	−563	−5.2	Mar 96	6.1	−34	−3.1
Jun 87	4.1	−537	−4.8	Jun 96	6.1	−703	−3.3
Sep 87	4.1	−1071	−4.9	Sep 96	6.2	−1673	−3.6
Dec 87	4.2	−862	−5.1	Dec 96	6.1	−1264	−3.9
Mar 88	4.8	100	−3.8	Mar 97	6.4	−879	−4.7
Jun 88	5.3	−182	−3.2	Jun 97	6.7	−2298	−6.3
Sep 88	6.2	−493	−2.2	Sep 97	6.8	−2305	−6.9
Dec 88	6.1	−169	−1.1	Dec 97	6.7	−1998	−7.6
Mar 89	7.0	285	−0.8	Mar 98	7.1	−473	−7.2
Graph	**9.3**	**9.4**	**9.4**	**Graph**	**9.3**	**9.4**	**9.4**

Index